AFRICAN NATIONALISM

by Ndabaningi Sithole

AFRICAN NATIONALISM

BY

NDABANINGI SITHOLE

WITH A FOREWORD BY
THE HON. R. S. GARFIELD TODD

CAPE TOWN
OXFORD UNIVERSITY PRESS
LONDON   NEW YORK
1959

Oxford University Press, Amen House, London E.C.4

GLASGOW   NEW YORK   TORONTO   MELBOURNE   WELLINGTON
BOMBAY   CALCUTTA   MADRAS   KARACHI   KUALA LUMPUR
CAPE TOWN   IBADAN   NAIROBI   ACCRA

⚓ PRINTED IN THE UNION OF SOUTH AFRICA BY
THE RUSTICA PRESS, PTY., LTD., WYNBERG, CAPE

FOREWORD

BY THE HON. R. S. GARFIELD TODD

African nationalism has already brought a great part of the continent under the government and control of black people, but, so far, the countries concerned have been populated almost exclusively by people of one race. African nationalism now clamours for control of multiracial countries such as the Union of South Africa, the Federation of Rhodesia and Nyasaland, and Kenya. The approximate ratio of Europeans to Africans in these countries is: the Union, 1 to 4; the Federation, 1 to 25; Kenya, 1 to 170. In our multiracial world, the struggle between European nationalism and African nationalism is watched with deep apprehension, and with the fervent hope that the conflicting forces may yet be aligned behind a new and compelling loyalty to the country instead of to the group.

Mr. Sithole's book is especially welcome and valuable at this time because it comes from a young African who has struggled against odds which would have dismayed most men. Now, with degrees from South Africa and from the United States of America, with a sensitiveness of nature which has made him fully aware of the handicaps and indignities which his own people face in the country of their birth, he believes that it is not only desirable but necessary, if the best interests of black and white are to be served, that people of all races should learn to respect one another and work together.

There will be criticisms from all sides, but anyone who really wishes to know what a moderate, capable, and thoughtful African thinks of the racial situation in southern Africa should read this book.

Salisbury
April 1959

ACKNOWLEDGEMENTS

Grateful acknowledgement is made to the following for permission to use extracts from the works cited:

Jonathan Cape Ltd., London, from *Report on Southern Africa* by Basil Davidson; Jonathan Cape Ltd., London, and Charles Scribner's Sons, New York, from *Cry, the Beloved Country* by Alan Paton; Cassell & Co. Ltd., London, from *Leopold the Unloved* by Ludwig Bauer; Harper & Brothers, New York, (four extracts) from *Inside Africa* by John Gunther, and (two extracts) from *Albert Schweitzer: An Anthology* by Charles R. Joy; La Page Internationale, Paris, and The John Day Company, Inc., New York, from *Revolt on the Nile* by Anwar El Sadat; the Houghton Mifflin Company, Boston, from *Race Relations* by Brewton Berry; the Houghton Mifflin Company, Boston, and William Collins Sons & Co. Ltd., London, from *African Giant* by Stuart Cloete; Thomas Nelson & Sons Ltd., Edinburgh, (two extracts) from *Ghana: Autobiography of Kwame Nkrumah*; the Oxford University Press, London, from *Ashanti Law and Constitution* by R. S. Rattray, and from *A Study of History*, Vol. 1, by Arnold J. Toynbee; the Princeton University Press, from *The Gold Coast in Transition* by David E. Apter; the Public Affairs Press, Washington, (three extracts) from *Egypt's Liberation: The Philosophy of the Revolution* by Gamal Abdul-Nasser; Routledge & Kegan Paul Ltd., London, (two extracts) from *The Laws and Customs of the Yoruba People* by A. K. Ajisafe; Charles Scribner's Sons, New York, and Mr. Alan Paton, from *South Africa in Transition* by Alan Paton; Martin Secker & Warburg Ltd., London, from *Facing Mount Kenya* by Jomo Kenyatta; Ronald M. Segal, editor of *Africa South*, from 'African Tragedy' in vol. 1, no. 3; D. van Nostrand Company, Inc., Princeton, N.J., (three extracts) from *Contemporary Africa: Continent in Transition* by T. Walter Wallbank (Anvil Series).

PUBLISHER'S NOTE

Events that have taken place in Africa since the end of 1957, when this book was completed, are not here described.

CONTENTS

CONTENTS

TO MY FAMILY

WIFE CANAAN (*Land of Milk and Honey*)

DAUGHTERS:
SIPIKELELO (*Perseverance*)
SIFISO (*Wish*)
SIKULULEKILE (*Freedom*)

AND SONS:
DINGINDLELA (*Find the Way*)
ZIBONELE (*Do It Yourself*)

CHAPTER ONE

Autobiographical Introduction

My father, Jim Sithole, at the age of 18, left Gazaland, his home district, to seek adventure and fortune in Umtali. He was only four months in Umtali when he decided to leave for Salisbury, where he worked as a 'kitchen boy' for two years. It was in Salisbury that he acquired a smattering of English and Afrikaans, which he could neither write nor read, just as he was unable to read or write any of the existing vernaculars of Southern Rhodesia. Allured by fortune stories told to him by his home boys who worked in Gwelo, he left Salisbury and found work with the Grand Hotel, Gwelo. Still spurred on by his love of adventure and fortune, he resigned his post and went to work in Bulawayo.

One fine morning as he was running an errand, an intelligent-looking country girl drew his attention. He halted, as he always says, 'to admire the killing beauty of this girl'. But the urgency of the errand demanded that he go on without stopping. He stood torn between his master's orders and his heart's desire. He soon forgot all about the errand and one and a half hours silently passed by unnoticed. He took all the particulars of this girl—her name Siyapi Tshuma, her home district Nyamandlovu. The girl was pleased that she had favourably impressed someone as handsome as my father.

Five visits to Nyamandlovu during week-ends soon rewarded my father's efforts. Six months after the engagement my father was married to Siyapi Tshuma according to native rites. On 21 July 1920, I was born to my father and mother—Siyapi Tshuma. I had a low mud-and-pole hut with a dirt floor for a maternity clinic, bits of old skins for my mattress, a reed mat for my bed, a goat's skin for my blanket, and a folded buck-skin for my pillow. On the same day that I arrived I was made to inhale the smoke from a burning goat's horn so that no evil would befall me. This smoking process was continued for three weeks and after that I was considered immune from all the evil intentions of our neighbours.

I grew up to the age of 7 playing hide-and-seek and making clay oxen. At night we gathered round granny to hear her tell us the wonderful stories of old. Granny was a thrilling story-teller, and it was not easy to forget her stories—so vivid, so appealing, so hair-raising, and told with such animation. She could tell a story, then introduce some singing, then continue the story, and even dance the story if it had some dancing in it. We could join the singing and the dancing. 'Behave yourself, or no story from granny' became a real warning that made us behave ourselves.

From 7 onwards my life was spent among bellowing bulls, lowing oxen, bleating sheep and goats, and baaing lambs. Herding was one of those irksome drudgeries. Like all other boys I disliked it. I envied men because they had done their stint. I longed to grow into a man quickly and be done with it.

There were many difficulties incidental to herding. Hunger was the commonest hardship. We had breakfast at about ten in the morning. Then we drove the cattle to the pasture, usually between five and ten miles away from home. Except for the wild fruit when in season, we did not have anything to eat until late in the evening. We made many silent prayers that the sun should set quickly so that we might return home to fill our empty bellies. We were not allowed to bring the cattle home before sunset. The next trouble came from the senior boys. They were the bosses and we, juniors, did all the hard work of herding. They gave orders and we carried them out. We were forbidden on pain of severe thrashing to disclose to people at home any unsavoury happening of the forest, which usually included senior boys' bullyism, cruelty and garden-raiding.

I remember one day when Zenzo, our senior boy, warned us, 'Don't tell anybody at home that we have taken water-melons from Menzelwa's garden'. We all promised not to. As we sat round the fire with some of our elders I proudly remarked to Zenzo, 'You thought we were going to tell the old people that we took some water-melons. You see, I haven't.' Poor me!

I learned the lesson the hard way. The next day every boy gave me some whipping on the legs saying, 'We don't say such things at home'. I pleaded, 'I will never do it again'.

One day as we were herding cattle, we saw a very strange thing. We thought it was a hut, but then it was moving very fast. In great fear we dashed into the forest near by, but curiosity checked our fear. We halted, and with panting hearts we carefully hid ourselves behind the bushes and made our observations from there. The strange moving hut then pulled up. 'It has seen us!' we cried in a chorus and rushed into the depths of the forest for dear life. Coming out through the other side of the forest we ran home as fast as our legs could carry us. Fearfully we reported the incident, and those who had been to Bulawayo and who had seen motor-cars nearly split their sides with laughter!

Like most of the children of our district, I had *amabetshu*—two skin aprons, one covering the back and the other the front. These *amabetshu* were tied round the waist so that they looked more like two rough triangular patches than clothing. The whole trunk remained bare. On cold days an old sack served as my overcoat, and on rainy days the same sack was used as a raincoat, by the simple method of pushing in one corner against the opposite corner so that the two corners stuck out at one point forming a kind of hood for my head. Round my neck was an *intebe*—a talisman, supposed to protect me from the evil spirits believed to dwell in the big dark forests of Nyamandlovu. Round my waist was yet another *intebe* supposed to protect me from the evil intentions of our neighbours. These articles constituted the entire stock of my clothing.

One chilly morning I accompanied my uncle to the dip-tank. The whole purpose of my going to the dip-tank was to see the white man who was said to be branding the cattle there. I had never seen a white face before. I was curious to see one. He was a tall, hefty, fearful figure. I grasped my uncle's arm firmly at the sight of this most extraordinary human being. His eyes moved quickly like those of a leopard we had seen one day. Everyone was paying attention to him. He was the master of the situation. Then he took a red-hot iron and pressed it on the cow's hind

3

quarters, and the cow made an eerie roar. I was terribly frightened. I never learned to like this branding white man who burnt good cows for sport.

At the end of 1930 my father left Nyamandlovu for Shabani. We walked all the way from Nyamandlovu to Bembesi Railway Station—a distance of about fifty miles. Father carried on his back Magwaza, my young brother, and mother carried Sinai on her back. I was old enough to walk the fifty miles. I was excited at the idea of seeing the train. I had never seen it before. It took us two days to get to Bembesi. There I awaited the arrival of the train with bated breath.

Father bought us clothes for the first time. We threw away our *amabetshu*. I struggled into my khaki shorts shaking with great excitement, and I endeavoured to put on my khaki shirt. At last the struggle was over. There I stood in my new clothes smiling excitedly and unable to believe that that was myself. I put my hands deep in my pockets like some important little man. We have never passed Bembesi without my wife, Canaan, insisting on my getting down and looking for my *amabetshu*.

'Puff! Puff! Puff! Puff!' came the sound from the distance. I became dead still with attention. Here now was the real thing the idea of which had greatly excited me, raised my hopes, whetted my sense of pleasure, eased my otherwise long and tedious journey, made me feel I was going to a better world, and made me forget all about granny and her stories. I listened fearfully to the terrifying noise; curiosity changed to fear, excitement to anxiety. I was bewildered and puzzled by this strange and terrific noise. I looked in the distance and out came the huge black monster 'vomiting' and 'coughing' great clouds of black smoke. It seemed to make straight for me. 'God! Save me from the monster!' I cried, dashing away from the monster. I was making for granny's home where no such threatening monsters dwelt. I longed for the peace and security in my granny's mud hut. I must have covered more than a quarter of a mile before father caught and carried me kicking and struggling. I would have jumped out of the train had he not prevented me. Fearfully I sat in the train and tightly held to my mother's arm. I became the centre of laughter, pity, and inquiry. I provided good sport for the passengers.

We reached Shabani in due course. The sight of row upon row of neatly thatched huts greatly impressed me. I had never seen anything like it before. Added to my bewilderment were the numerous tribes in this compound. They spoke different languages and observed different customs. Among these were the Makaranga, the Vazezuru, the Vamanyika, the Mashangana, the Manyasa, the Macawa, the Masena, the Marubare and a few other tribes. Fortune-hunting had brought them all together.

Life was comparatively easy here. There was no herding. We spent most of our time playing in and around the compound, visiting local stores, exploring workshops, sliding down the big asbestos dumps, digging holes in the old and solid dumps, and on Saturdays and Sundays we acted as caddies for European golfers. It was such great fun that I soon forgot all about Nyamandlovu and granny's thrilling stories told by the fireside.

In this compound there was a school run by the British Methodist Church (then called Wesleyan Church). In 1932 I started going to school. I went to school because I had nothing else to do, and because I thought it was a good thing to do what other children were doing. Our lessons were the usual three Rs, Bible, hygiene, vegetable-gardening, clay-modelling and simple woodwork.

We had a very strict teacher who did not spare his whip if he thought we needed it. He used the whip to get us to master the lesson quickly and thoroughly, to make us quiet when we were noisy, to get good attendance and to make us come to school at the right time. There was magic in our teacher's whip. It achieved exactly what he wanted.

My father was not interested in my schooling, but my mother was. She had gone to school only for two weeks before she revolted against her teacher's constant whipping and quit the school. That was the only time she went to school.

Despite our teacher's constant whippings we liked our school. Learning and whipping became inseparable. We all accepted the

5

fact that without whipping there could be no real learning. Whipping was the order of the day.

At the end of 1932, following the persistent advice of my father, I left school and went to work for a Mr. Bell. I was employed as a 'kitchen boy'. I used to look after their five-year-old boy. Mrs. Bell taught me how to wash myself regularly, how to clean my clothes and my teeth, keep my finger-nails short and clean and how to keep her Charlie clean. For the slightest dirt she saw she flared up. Sometimes I honestly believed she was mad. 'If the dirt is mine, what business has she to worry about it?' I often wondered.

In 1935 I received a letter from a cousin of mine, London Sithole, who was five years my junior. The letter had been written in English. Although I had continued my schooling by attending night school, I had not progressed beyond the Sub B grade. I could not read the letter; my pride was deeply injured. 'I can't read what a young boy writes!' I cried in sheer disgust. The thought of being surpassed by someone five years younger than I was was unbearable. It stung my soul, and for weeks, as we say in Ndebele, 'it ate me from inside'. I decided to go to the same boarding-school where London was. At the end of July, after many pleas from my house-mistress that I should not go away, I was finally released.

'I want to go to school', I told my father.

'You lazy, fellow. Go back and work', he growled. Then he reminded me of the many kindnesses that Mrs. Hatfield had shown me, and told me that he would have preferred me to die in her service. 'Tomorrow,' he said, biting his teeth with indignation, 'you go back to Mrs. Hatfield and work. I don't want to hear anything about your school.'

I knew my father had spoken and that he would not take back what he had said. 'Yes, father', I agreed with him.

'That's a boy', he said softening down.

The next morning I got all my clothes and blankets ready. Instead of going to Mrs. Hatfield's house I found myself going to Dadaya Mission by train.

'Did you apply?' asked the missionary-in-charge at Dadaya

6

1

Mission. This was the Rev. Garfield Todd, later the Prime Minister of Southern Rhodesia.

'No, Nkosi', I said.

'This is August, my son,' he said sadly, 'and we take pupils at the beginning of the year.'

I was dumb, puzzled, disappointed and I felt tears in my eyes. In sheer pity for me, however, the missionary accepted me. The headmistress, Mrs. Grace Todd, placed me in Standard One. I had saved money but not more than £2. Fees were only 10s. a year! I paid in my fees and I became a boarder. Now perhaps my wounded pride would heal up!

I was behind in many things. My arithmetic was atrocious, my written English was bad although my oral English and English reading were not so bad. I had been used to answering those in authority as 'Yes, Nkosi' or 'Yes, Missus', but now I had to learn the new way of saying 'Yes, Mfundisi' or 'Yes, Nkosi-kazi'. I used to mix up the old and the new way, to the great amusement of both staff and students.

Life here was very interesting in many ways. There were the Christian Endeavour Society, the Debating Society, the camp-fires and Sunday services. All these things were very interesting to me. In the classroom we were taught the usual three Rs and the other subjects. We liked classroom work better than outside work. We erroneously held to the view that education meant exemption from all forms of manual work; to us education meant reading books, writing and talking English, and doing arithmetic. We thought that the ability to do these things was the only true education. To use one's hands to earn one's living, we thought, was below one's dignity. We resented all forms of manual work.

Perhaps an explanation of our attitude to manual work is not out of place here. At our homes we had done a lot of ploughing, planting, weeding and harvesting; we had hewn wood and drawn water; we had tended sheep, goats and cattle; we had done a hundred and one odd jobs. We knew how to do these things. We had come to school, not for these, but for those things we did not know. What we knew was not education;

7

education was what we did not know. If we had had our way we would have unanimously voted for 'Only classroom work, and no manual work'. We wanted, as we said in Ndebele, 'to learn the book until it remained in our heads, to speak English until we could speak it through our noses'.

The missionary here was ideally suited for handling boys of our dispositions. By his own example and precept he taught us the dignity of manual labour. He used his own hands in the fields, in his own back yard, and he washed his own car. He moulded bricks with us, hoed the fields with us, and did many odd jobs with us. Gradually our attitude toward manual work changed for the better.

The same year that I was admitted to Dadaya Mission, I professed repentance and acceptance of Christ. I did not accept Christ as a personal Redeemer, or because of a deep conviction of Christ's way, but because I thought that since other boys and girls had accepted Him, it would be a nice thing for me to do the same thing. Not to be baptized was a kind of social stigma that goaded many boys and girls into professed repentance. Christ to me meant no more and no less than a social badge.

In 1936 my little savings were exhausted and I was compelled to remain on the Mission Station working holiday after holiday. It was not an easy thing to remain on the Mission Station every holiday. It was a great stigma as it revealed the poor financial circumstances of my parents. Youthful pride that refuses to accept disagreeable facts about one's poor parents, and chooses to paint one's poor parents in brighter colours than they really are, made me feel sharply what it meant to be born of poor parents. Like all others who were in the same boat with me, I was held in great contempt but I soon got used to the game. I knew only too well that going home meant no school fees and that this meant no schooling, but I liked schooling.

During this time several girls came to Dadaya Mission to seek refuge. These girls had been pledged, or forced into marriage, by their own parents. Refusing to marry where they did not love, they deserted their parents and took refuge on the Mission

Station. The missionary-in-charge befriended them and cared for them.

'But are you going to receive *lobola* for these girls?' I asked him one day.

'No, but why?' he asked me.

'Well, I see you care for them as well as if you are going to get something from them', I said.

'No, I won't get a farthing, Ndabaningi.'

'But why all this bother then?'

'I am doing it for Christ's sake.'

'Christ's sake!' I cried. 'What's that?'

'Well, Christ wants everyone to be free, to marry whom they choose, not to be forced. I'm doing this because I want to do Christ's will. That is why I am a Christian.'

This was news to me. I, too, decided to help others without expecting anything in return. Here again I was just aping the great missionary, but I was growing in my Christian experience.

In 1937 the missionary-in-charge asked me to help him in the dispensary. I gladly helped him for the next three years. I noticed that the missionary lived for all those in need of help. If there was any case of illness and it came to his notice he would attend to it immediately. Sometimes when I was overworked I felt like telling him so, but I was ashamed to tell him so because he was more overworked than I was.

Fire-burns were the worst cases that we had to deal with. One day a woman brought her baby over whom a boiling pot had tipped. That little baby, hardly two months old, was a frightful and repulsive spectacle. She died in my hands while I was trying to help her. Another charming little girl a little over 4 years of age, had all her abdomen burnt. Her drunken mother had been cooking *sadza* while she lay by the fire. The pot tipped over and the porridge spilled on the girl. She died within eight hours of admission. All these things kept the missionary busy. 'For Christ's sake', he kept on saying as he went about helping these people. Gradually I began to see and my faith grew from mere imitation to something real.

From my limited Christian experience, I have come to

realize that Christ's way of life is something that grows from within. It is not something that grows on the individual. First we see our need for a Saviour, and after letting Him in, we begin to grow like Him as we see Him in the Bible or lived by other lives. I began to realize that to accept Christ was to allow the gradual unfolding of a nobler purpose as manifested in Christ's life. The Sunday School also helped me in getting a real Christian experience and fellowship.

In 1939 I finished my Standard Six at Dadaya Mission. I was highest in my class. I was awarded a Beit Bursary of £10 tenable at Waddilove Training Institution for two years. I would have left school if this award had not been made, unless someone else had come to my aid.

In many ways Waddilove was a stimulating place. There were several departments—building, carpentry, theology, teacher training, and the Central Primary School. The Rev. George Hay Pluke was the principal of the school and under him fell the departmental heads. Our professional teacher in the Teacher Training Department was Mr. William Tregidgo. We all admired him. He was strict and thorough, fair and firm, and demanded the same from us. By his own example he taught us to be punctual. It is exactly thirteen years since he taught us, and through the corridors of time and space I can still hear him saying slowly in his clear bell-like voice, 'Hammer it, and hammer it, and hammer it, into the children's minds'.

Our teacher for principles of education was the Rev. George Hay Pluke. Mr. Pluke was opposed to any form of corporal punishment, and he taught us not to use it. We did not agree with him. At home old people had not spared the rod to spoil the children; at my previous Central Primary School whipping had been used as part of disciplining the students. Apparently, I had come out the better for it. I warmly supported corporal punishment, and as most of us were no adherents of the 'no-whip' theory, we secretly thrashed the children we taught during our practical teaching periods.

Mr. Pluke was very interested in cultural reading. 'The trouble with you, Ndabaningi, is that you always read for

examinations and not for pleasure. Learn to read for pleasure.'
Sometimes I nearly told him, 'Pleasure won't make me pass'.
But I soon caught on to what he meant. He laid good foundations
for my cultural reading. Under his directions and encouragement
I read over fifty books during my two years at Waddilove—
English classics mostly: *David Copperfield, Oliver Twist, Silas
Marner, The Vicar of Wakefield, The Last Days of Pompeii, Prester
John*, and others in their simplified and abridged forms.

At Waddilove Sunday School we were led by Miss Marjorie
Baker, who was very devoted to spiritual matters. I was one of
her Sunday School teachers. She taught us during preparation
classes to pray hard over lessons before we taught them. She
taught us the value of strictly private prayers.

When I finished my teaching course at Waddilove I was sent
to a kraal school where I taught lower classes. My head was
buzzing with private studies. I wanted more education. If I had
had money I would have gone to a secondary school. Amid most
forbidding surroundings I did my private studies side by side with
my teaching. I was glad that a year of real hard work rewarded
me with National Junior Certificate. In those days, particularly
the first half of the 1940's, the possession of such academic qualifications was a rare achievement. After my success more teachers
enrolled for National Junior Certificate. They were no longer
content to be spectators.

One day as I went about my teaching, I lost my temper with
one of my Standard Two girls who always came late to school
and always smiled whenever I told her not to smile; she did not
seem to care about the matter. I had punished her but there was
no apparent reform. I was reluctant to proceed to corporal
punishment, not because I had believed what Mr. Pluke had tried
to teach us, but because I was young and I feared the reactions
of the girl's father, who had the evil repute of a witchdoctor. But
in my anger—that temporary madness—I soundly thrashed the
girl.

'Teacher, you will die!' cried many children in pity for me.
'You'll die! You'll die!' They were all death-scared. What strong
hold witchcraft has on the minds of the people! Children grow

up in it and it is almost impossible to dissuade them against witch-craft when they grow old.

Late in the afternoon the girl's father came. He was a tall, muscular man, not less than six feet. He looked contemptuously at me. I felt heavily his presence.

'Why did you beat my daughter?' he asked.

I tried to explain as best I could, but he would not listen.

'You won't see the next harvest', he threatened.

By this statement he meant that he was going to invoke his evil spirits which would see to it that I was put out of existence mysteriously. I knew what he meant. I had heard numerous stories of his nocturnal duties. He had bewitched men, women, and children in the neighbourhood. Educated and uneducated, Christian and heathen, young and old, rich and poor, all believed implicitly that this man had supernatural power over human life. I had never been threatened in this way before. I felt uneasy although I had never believed in mysterious killing by witch-doctors.

Providence has equipped each of us with something to defend us in time of real need. I quietly said to myself, 'If it means death, then it is death. I must face it like a man.' I faced the disagreeable facts of my possible death before the next harvest.

'Yes, I hear you, Father', I said turning to the man. 'I die before the next harvest, but you won't see your family tonight. I'm sorry you did not bid them farewell. They will never see you again.'

'What!' he cried sneering at me. 'How can a kid like you know such deep things of life?'

'Do you think I was born of a tree? I have a father, a grand-father and a chain of ancestors. I die before next harvest and you today.'

'I was just playing, my boy.'

'No playing. You are a man; you have spoken. I am a man; I have spoken. What men have spoken can't be unspoken.'

Silence and stillness fell upon him and I emerged the master of the situation. He was gradually becoming the victim of the situation he had created.

'Forgive me, son of Sithole', he pleaded.

After many pretended refusals I forgave him and told him to go home.

'I can't go home alone now, son of Sithole. It's getting dark. Accompany me, please', he said.

I went into my bedroom and got my black walking-stick and then I led the way along a narrow winding path and he followed behind. With my walking-stick I hit the darkness right and left. 'No, boys, don't seize the man. He's our friend.' As I said this I ran behind him and chased away my imaginary boys, giving them a good talking-to. For two miles the poor man was silent with fear and I spoke again and again to my imaginary spooks.

He believed without any shadow of doubt that I was a witch-doctor and that I possessed many evil spirits in the forest. This greatly improved school and church attendance!

When I was transferred to Dadaya Mission to teach Standard Five there, I found that many teachers were very keen to do private studies. Mr. Todd volunteered to take them in some subjects and I also volunteered to take them in others. They were very keen in their lessons. Side by side with my teaching work I also read for my Matriculation Exemption Certificate. I would have saved money to go for my university training, but I had three sisters to educate so I had to content myself with private study.

In 1946 I got married and 1947 brought us a baby girl and some real domestic trouble. My mother insisted that we smoke the baby, and I refused. I told her that since I was a Christian and an educated man I could not do that. Then she would count on her fingers some outstanding Christians and educated people who smoked their children and tied *intebe* round their waists. She argued that unless the baby was treated by the witchdoctors she would die. Finally she told me that with or without my consent she would smoke the child and call in a local witchdoctor to treat the baby.

'You can't do things like that with my baby, mother', I protested.

'That's not your baby. The baby belongs to the whole Sithole

13

family. When you were born I smoked you. All your sisters and brothers were smoked. I have now nine children all smoked. No baby ever lives unless it is smoked.'

She had the support of almost everyone, but I insisted that no such thing was going to be done to the baby. Canaan was inclined to listen to the voice of experience rather than to that of a new-comer in matrimony.

I rudely said to both my mother and my mother-in-law, 'We didn't plan that the baby was going to be female, or to be what she is. Someone did that. The same person will continue to look after the baby. I had no voice in my own creation.'

My mother-in-law remarked, 'My son, you have wonderful faith'.

'It's not faith,' retorted my mother sourly, 'it's childishness.'

1948 found me at Tegwane Training Institution, where I was employed as an assistant method master to Miss Dora Warwick, who was the method mistress and Headmistress of the Teacher Training Department. I learnt many things from Miss Warwick. Her great energies well fitted her for the hard task of dealing with all kinds of boys and girls.

I went through a course of Bible study after which I became an accredited local preacher of the British Methodist Church. I attended regularly the local Y.M.C.U. group and my eyes were opened to the great desire among boys and girls to preach the Gospel and testify. I enjoyed preaching at the Plumtree jail. I had never done this before, and it had never occurred to my mind that people in jail were worth preaching to. There was something in the prisoners' singing which deeply touched me. I was left in no doubt that most of them were not beyond the point of redemption. I became engrossed in preaching to them. Despite the austere atmosphere of the prison-cells, the prisoners had not lost their sense of humour.

The Rev. Mr. Chapman said one day, 'Brother, what about the ministry?' And as usual I tried to evade the question. My cousin, the Rev. O. D. Ramushu, said to me another day, 'Why don't you join the ministry?' As usual I hesitated to make a reply. Then he went on in his blunt way, 'You fear there's not much in the ministry, eh?' I was interested in the ministry but something held me back.

At the end of 1950 I left Tegwane and joined a newly organized church. I now had an opportunity of preaching. For the first time in my life I saw with my own eyes how gospel-starved the people were in the rural areas away from mission stations. Great crowds came if they heard that I was going to preach to them. People were interested in studying the simple word of God in the Bible. We had fewer workers, but more people to preach to. I had never ridden the bicycle so much before. I was on my 'gospel bicycle' nearly every week-end after classes on Friday for places between ten and twenty-five miles away from my school. I did this for two years. The Rev. E. T. J. Nemapare tried to make arrangements for me to train as a minister, but owing to financial difficulties he could not. Soon the poor financial circumstances of the young church made it very difficult for both my wife and me to continue our services there.

We joined the Mt. Silinda teaching staff in 1953. The first sermon I preached at Mt. Silinda made a good impression, and ever after the Rev. Frank Meacham used to say to me, 'Ndabaningi, you are not a teacher. Your place is in the ministry. I am not joking. I mean it.'

I must mention here some of my inner struggles with regard to God's work. Although I started preaching at the age of 18, I did not think of taking up preaching as full-time service. I always argued with my disturbing soul that I was a teacher by profession and that preaching was all right for me as a part-time job. Many a time I had felt something stirring my conscience, but I dreaded to make the move. Sometimes I thought it was older people's work. But all these were excuses to soothe my troubled conscience. This struggle continued well over eight years. To be or not to be a full-time worker for Christ worried me; Canaan said to me one day, as we sat discussing the question, 'If God intends you for a full-time worker, don't worry about deciding now. We can't vote on the matter today. He'll work out His Way for you.' I dismissed the matter for the next four years although the thing kept on coming back to me from time to time.

I had decided to evade the call by being silent about it. I contented myself with teaching as my full-time job and preaching as part-time.

One evening I mentioned again the matter to Canaan. 'Yes, I know the thing is always worrying you. It's there, I can see.'

'But I can't go and train as a minister now. We've three children.' I tried to excuse my reluctance about obeying the call.

'You looked after Phike while I went for training', said Canaan. 'It's my turn now to look after the children while you go for training.'

'Three years!' I cried.

'Why not? I know you'll never be happy until you satisfy this thing in you. When we got married I found you talking about it. It's seven years now since then and you are still talking about it.'

We invited Miss Lindile Nyembezi to our house one evening. She was one of the old Zulu missionaries who had come to Gazaland for the spreading of Christ's Gospel. I told her the story of my troubles. For a long time she prayed and kept on repeating. 'Show him the way. . . . If it is monetary consideration holding him back . . . good Lord, show him the way. If it is an anticipated evil that makes him not surrender himself to Thee . . . good Lord, show him the way.'

Then Canaan prayed. I had never heard her pray like that before. 'If it is Thy will, Lord, that he give all his time for Thee, help him to decide.' At times she was overcome with weeping. The whole atmosphere was tense.

After both Canaan and Miss Nyembezi had prayed the three of us sat in silence for some time.

I felt greatly strengthened. I decided to see our local minister, the Rev. Elija Mwadira. I told him about my strong call to the Christian ministry, and I expressed the view that I feared to make any formal application to the Church as I was a new man at the place and that after three or four years I would make one.

'If the call is there,' said the Rev. Mr. Mwadira, 'make it now. Say it so that we know it is there.' After a long prayer he advised me to go and see the Rev. John Heinrich in connexion with my call.

Following the Rev. Mr. Mwadira's advice, I went to see both the Rev. Mrs. Heinrich and the Rev. J. Heinrich. They were interested in my story, and the Rev. J. Heinrich solemnly said, 'I am convinced of your Christian conviction. We have sensed that since you came here.' He advised me as to the proper procedure. Both Mr. and Mrs. Heinrich prayed.

After this I went to Miss Ivy Craig, a very close friend of mine who regards me as her grandson and our children as her grandchildren. I told her. She was touched, and she simply said, 'We have been praying for such things'. She started an evening Bible discussion group which has broadened my Christian outlook and deepened my Christian experience. Like Mr. and Mrs. Heinrich she always endeavoured to surround me with Christian literature.

The only thing that remained now was to make my application to the Church Association and the Mission Council. I drafted the application and called Miss Nyembezi and Canaan. I read it to them. Miss Nyembezi prayed fervently and wept. Then Canaan prayed and also wept. I could feel that these women had completely surrendered themselves to God. There was something better felt than expressed in words. 'If the thing worrying you, my son,' said Miss Nyembezi, 'is of God, then He'll answer you.'

I duly dispatched the application to the Superintendent of Churches and I received the following reply:

Dear Mr. Sithole,

. . . I wish to thank you for this letter. It is inspiring to receive such a letter, and one does not receive this kind of letter very often.

We are grateful to God who has placed this desire within your heart. I know that He will guide you and us as we give your request most sympathetic and thoughtful consideration. . . .

May God be very near to you and give His own guidance for the future as to what is best for you and the Mission here. I personally hope that it will be possible for you to take theological training and serve Christ in this Field in the years to come.

Signed: John Marsh (Superintendent of Churches).

A meeting of the Church Association was held at the end of

the year. My application was presented and Mr. E. J. Mlambo, the devoted worker for the welfare of the public, regarded the application as the answer to their long prayers. 'At last God has answered us', he said. The application was unanimously accepted. The Mission Council, which is the supreme body of the American Board Mission of Southern Rhodesia, unanimously approved of the application.

A sermon I had preached at Mt. Silinda Institute on 'Our Need of Love and Not Weapons' was sent by Miss Craig to the Secretary for Africa, of the American Board, Boston. This was at the time of race trouble in Durban. She thought the secretary might like such material to counteract adverse conceptions in the minds of people in America. The result was that it kindled an interest and opened the way for study in America.

.   .   .

I did my secondary education and my Bachelor of Arts Degree entirely by private study and correspondence. When I look back to the most discouraging surroundings among which I grew up, I cannot escape the feeling that 'I am one of the chosen vessels', and in gratitude to God who has been so gracious to me I raise my voice:

> 'From sinking sands, He lifted me;
> With tender hands, He lifted me;
> From shades of night to plains of light,
> O, praise His name, He lifted me.'

CHAPTER TWO

After World War II

The average white man in Africa is scared almost out of his senses by the rapidly emerging African nationalism. An African nationalist is regarded not only as potential but as real danger to the present status of the white man in Africa. The question has been often asked: What is it that has brought about this strong nationalistic feeling among the otherwise docile peoples of Africa who had, to all appearance, acquiesced in white domination?

It would be idle to single out one factor as causative of this new vigorous African nationalism sweeping the length and breadth of the vast continent of Africa, the home of approximately 140,000,000 blacks, 65,000,000 Arabs, and 5,000,000 whites. Like all movements, African nationalism roots back into history, and without this historical foundation, the seemingly sudden African nationalism becomes inexplicable. There are chain causes which may be traced back to pre-European days of Africa. In our examination of the factors that have given rise to this much-talked-about African nationalism, it is well to bear in mind that all movements of consequence are preceded by ideas.

World War II, as many people have frequently noted, has had a great deal to do with the awakening of the peoples of Africa. During the war the African came in contact with practically all the peoples of the earth. He met them on a life-and-death-struggle basis. He saw the so-called civilized and peaceful and orderly white people mercilessly butchering one another just as his so-called savage ancestors had done in tribal wars. He saw no difference between the primitive and the civilized man. In short, he saw through European pretensions that only Africans were savages. This had a revolutionizing psychological impact on the African.

But more than this, World War II taught the African most powerful ideas. During the war the Allied Powers taught the subject peoples (and millions of them!) that it was not right for Germany to dominate other nations. They taught the subject peoples to fight and die for freedom rather than live and be subjugated by Hitler. The subject peoples learned the lesson well and responded magnificently, and they fought, and endured hardship, and died, under the magic spell of freedom.

During the war the British officers appealed to the Africans to join the armed services, and so they began extensive propaganda against the Nazis. The British were not the only ones who did this; practically all the Allied powers did the same thing. The following story typifies well the attitude of the African and other subject peoples.

'Away with Hitler! Down with him!' said the British officer.

'What's wrong with Hitler?' asked the African.

'He wants to rule the whole world', said the British officer.

'What's wrong with that?'

'He is German, you see', said the British officer, trying to appeal subtly to the African's tribal consciousness.

'What's wrong with his being German?'

'You see,' said the British officer, trying to explain in terms that would be conceivable to the African mind, 'it is not good for one tribe to rule another. Each tribe must rule itself. That's only fair. A German must rule Germans, an Italian, Italians, and a Frenchman, French people.'

But the extremely wary British officer did not say, 'A Briton, Britons'. What he said, however, carried weight with the Africans who rallied in thousands under the British Flag. They joined the war to end the threat of Nazi domination.

After World War II, the Africans began to direct their British-aroused anti-domination spirit against the Allied powers who had extensive colonial empires in Africa. (And the Asiatics did the same thing against colonial powers.) Various moves were made by Africans to end British and French dominance in Africa. 'You said it was wrong for the Germans to rule the world. It is also wrong for the British to dominate Africans', became the attitude of many an African who had long been dreaming of the return of Africa to her rightful owners.

Perhaps it will clarify our discussion if we trace briefly the African nationalist movement for full independence after the last World War. This nationalist movement was not confined to Africa; and to understand the African situation better, it will reward us to put Africa aside for a moment and visit the gigantic continent of Asia and the Pacific Islands.

During and after the war new fully independent Asiatic nations were born. In the Near East, Israel, Lebanon, and Syria became independent republics. In Asia, India and Pakistan won their independence from Britain in 1947. Ceylon and Burma won theirs from the same power in 1948. The U.S.A. granted the Philippine Islands their independence in 1946. Indonesia shook off the Dutch yoke in 1950.

It is noteworthy here that after the war millions of people were liberated from the clutches of colonial powers. This is to say millions of people overthrew, by peaceful means or by armed revolution, alien domination. The whole atmosphere became laden with the spirit of independence, and as it is the nature of the air to circulate, it soon reached Africa, and from Cape to Cairo the African peoples are breathing in this wonderful breeze of independence. Naturally, the newly-won independence of many subject peoples of the earth has been a powerful impetus in the emergence of African nationalism.

On the continent of Africa, after long, uninterrupted and undisputed colonial rule by European powers, new African nations, with full independence, are making their appearance. Liberia, which is the oldest independent African State, has been the envy of many European-dominated African countries. These other independent African countries, Ethiopia, Libya, Egypt, Tunisia, Morocco, South Africa, Sudan, and Ghana, thrill and excite other African countries which are still under European domination. There is, all over Africa, a chain reaction for independence, and this is just the beginning of African liberation from European domination.

Perhaps quoting from some of the outstanding African political leaders will serve to make clear what we are trying to say here. Colonel Nasser says:

'We cannot, under any circumstances, remain aloof from the terrible and sanguinary struggle going on in Africa today between five million whites and 200 million Africans. . . . The peoples of Africa will continue to look at us, who guard the northern gate and constitute their link with all the outside world. We will never . . . be able to relinquish our responsibility to support, with all our might, the spread of enlightenment and civilization to the remotest depth of the jungle. . . .

'The Dark Continent is now the scene of a strange and excited turbulence. . . . We shall not, in any circumstances, stand idly by in the face of what is going on in Africa in the belief that it will not affect or concern us. . . .

'I will continue to dream of the day when I will find in Cairo a great African Institute dedicated . . . to an enlightened African consciousness, and to sharing with others from all over the world in the work of advancing the peoples of the continent.'[1]

Different African leaders may word their aspirations to, and dream of, full African independence differently, but the spirit is basically the same as that of the Egyptians—namely, that African countries must help one another in their struggle to overthrow foreign domination.

Dr. Kwame Nkrumah, the Prime Minister of the then Gold Coast, now Ghana, said, in 1949:

'Freedom for the Gold Coast will be a fountain of inspiration from which other African colonial territories can draw when the time comes for them to strike for their freedom. An independent Gold Coast will encourage the remaining dependent territories of Africa to continue their struggle for freedom and independence. . . . To me, independence for the Gold Coast is meaningless unless it is linked up with the total liberation of the continent of Africa.'[2]

Even on the day that the Gold Coast gained her full independence from Britain, though remaining within the British Commonwealth of Nations, Prime Minister Kwame Nkrumah still reminded the sixty-six nations represented at the Ghana

[1] *Egypt's Liberation: The Philosophy of the Revolution* (Public Affairs Press, Washington), pp. 109–11.   [2] *Phylon*, Fourth Quarter, 1955, p. 407.

Freedom celebrations that Ghana 'would assist all African peoples in their pursuit of freedom and social progress'.[1]

An Asiatic once said to me, 'We owe our independence to Adolf Hitler!'

Needless to say, Adolf Hitler was not in any way committed to a programme of liberating downtrodden people, but rather committed to a plan of world domination. But my Asiatic friend's paradoxical statement meant this, that during World War II, the subject peoples were taught how to resist domination with their very lives, and this lesson would not have been so thoroughly taught and so well mastered in the absence of the threatening militaristic and imperialistic Nazi regime. The big lesson learned was—DOMINATION BY ANY NATION IS WRONG—and this is still echoing throughout the world, and it is being reinforced in many quarters in and outside Africa.

Here then is the paradox of history, that the Allied powers, by effectively liquidating the threat of Nazi world domination, set in motion those powerful forces which are now liquidating, with equal effectiveness, European domination in Africa. As a Moroccan put it, 'Our struggle against France is a carry-over of the same struggle against Hitler'. The emergence and the march of African nationalism are in reality a boomerang on the colonial powers. They fired the anti-domination bullet at Nazi Germany, but now the same bullet is being fired at them!

Unfortunately the outside world, that is the Western world, do not seem to see this African nationalism in its right perspective. They think it is an anti-white movement, and therefore they are not sympathetic to it. Many African nationalists have been branded as rebels and subjected to the severest penalties for their nationalist activities.

In India, for instance, Mahatma Gandhi, the perfecter of the passive-resistance weapon, became a regular jailbird for his nationalist activities which brought about full independence for more than 360,000,000 people. Nationalist Prime Minister Nehru was another illustrious Indian jailbird. In Morocco nationalist Sultan Mohammed V was deposed by France in 1953, and exiled

[1] *The Christian Science Monitor*, 6 March 1957.

23

to Madagascar, but the nationalist struggle kept going on until France was obliged to grant Morocco full independence. Prime Minister Kwame Nkrumah of the new Ghana was imprisoned for his nationalist activities which were construed by the then British administration to be seditious. What all this adds up to is that Westerners become so hateful of the African nationalists that any African nationalist is usually regarded as the hater of the white man.

This view, though widely prevalent, is nevertheless wrong. African nationalism is directed against European domination, and not against the white man, just as Canada, Australia, New Zealand, and South Africa wanted their full independence from Britain, but without repudiating friendship with Britain. What these members of the Commonwealth of Nations wanted was the removal of the domination of the United Kingdom Government. They wanted to manage their own affairs in their own country. What the African wants is not to drive away the white man, but to have his full independence. It is unfortunate that the African's move against European domination is interpreted as his hatred of the white man. When the Allied powers moved against Nazi Germany, it was not because they hated the Germans but because they hated German domination. The Allied powers did not set themselves against the German people but against German domination. Similarly, African nationalism is a move against European domination which tends to devalue the African people. The African hates European domination but does not hate the white man. He welcomes him. The physical presence of the white man in Africa is welcome, but his domination is unwelcome.

Perhaps we should state how it comes about that most whites conceive the plausible but erroneous idea that in general African nationalism is aimed at the white people. The average white man in Africa equates his existence with white domination. He seems convinced that he can only thrive in Africa on domination. In other words, domination and the white man have come to be regarded by the white man himself as two sides of the same coin. European existence has become inextricably interwoven with white domination so that the average white man cannot see how

24

he can live in Africa without it. It has become his very breath of life, and he who sets himself against white domination logically sets himself against the white man. To try to choke white domination is like trying to choke the white man himself, and hence the white opposition to African nationalism.

But, of course, there is all the difference between the white man and white domination, although the average white man is so used to riding on the shoulders of Africans that he cannot be persuaded to believe that he can still live and move and have his being in Africa after the Africans have thrown him off their shoulders. There is room enough for many people who desire to live on equal footing. The 'domination space' in Africa is rapidly shrinking.

Talking to a University of Life Forum, in Newburyport, Massachusetts, in November 1956, I tried, in the course of my address, to show that, 'Africa needs the friendship of the West, and the West the friendship of Africa. But while this is perfectly true, it is also equally true that Africa does not need, and does not want, the domination of the West, just as the West does not want African domination.'

To illustrate further that African nationalism opposes, not the white man, but white domination, we wish to quote once more from Prime Minister Kwame Nkrumah of Ghana: 'I stand for no racialism, no discrimination against any race or individual, but I am unalterably opposed to imperialism in any form.'

'What we stand against', said a Rhodesian African politician, 'is not the white man, but this obnoxious practice of subordinating Africans to European interests so that they [Africans] become things to be manipulated by the white man according to the whims of his temper. We want to be accepted as men by men of other races.'

In South Africa where the Nationalist Party in power is determined to retain domination over non-whites, a new spirit among both black and white is pressing for a new independence for the downtrodden peoples of that land. In July 1955 the Congress of the People composed of some 3,000 people was convened and a Freedom Charter was adopted. The Charter ran:

'We, the people of South Africa, declare for all our country and the world to know: that South Africa belongs to all who live in it, black and white, and that no government can justly claim authority unless it is based on the will of all the people; that our people have been robbed of their birthright to land, liberty, and peace by a form of government founded on injustice and inequality; that our country will never be prosperous or free until all our people live in brotherhood, enjoying equal rights and opportunities; that only a democratic state, based on the will of all the people, can secure to all their birthright without distinction of colour, race, sex, or belief; and therefore, we the people of South Africa, black and white together—equals, countrymen, and brothers—adopt this Freedom Charter. And we pledge ourselves to strive together, sparing nothing of our strength and courage, until the democratic changes here set out have been won.'[1]

The Reverend George Gay, an American Negro historian with a very keen insight into the course of human history, has said:

'The last World War did not teach the subject peoples the spirit of independence. This was already there. People had long felt the poignant injustice of subordination and discrimination. They had no means hitherto of vocalizing and dramatizing their deep-seated grievances. World War II focused these grievances more intensely and gave them an effective expression. World War II did not give birth to the spirit of independence, but rather gave expression to that spirit which was already there. Pre-World War II conditions broke down the high walls of European domination, and hence what was all along there is now vigorously flowing out trying to find its own level. World War II was a very powerful instrument in forestalling Nazi world domination, and it has been equally effective in ringing the death-bell of European colonialism.'

T. Walter Wallbank says:

'The two decades separating World War I from World

[1] 'Treason in South Africa', an article by George M. Houser in *The Christian Century*, 6 March 1957, as quoted therein, p. 289.

War II were formative years of African nationalism. On the surface, little was to be seen, but pressures and aspirations were building up that broke loose with astonishing force following the end of hostilities in 1945. . . .

'If the seeds of African nationalism were sown in the two decades between wars, they matured with astonishing speed after 1939. A number of factors explain this growth. To justify their cause the Allied nations, such as Britain, France and the United States, promised to speed up the tempo of self-government for Colonial powers.'[1]

[1] Wallbank: *Contemporary Africa: Continent in Transition*, Anvil Series (D. van Nostrand, Princeton), pp. 51, 59.

CHAPTER THREE

White Supremacy and African Nationalism

The next factor which we shall discuss is what is popularly called 'White Supremacy'. Let it be noted from the beginning, that, in general terms, the doctrine of white supremacy represents the sum total of European attitudes towards the African people.

An outstanding Rhodesian African politician defined white supremacy as 'the white man's keep-down-the-nigger policy'. A Kenya African defined it as 'the rule-by-might doctrine'. Many Africans equate it with Hitler's Aryan doctrine. A Nigerian African once said, 'There are two dangers to the peace of the world—Communism and white supremacy. Both are based on the same principles; both employ the same methods; both aim at the same thing—domination of others.' He went on, 'White supremacy is to us [Africans] as Russian Communism is to Russia's satellite countries.'

An African teacher from Northern Rhodesia expressed his views thus:

'I don't hate white supremacy because it is white. I hate it because it is designed for my domination and humiliation. It hurts me. White supremacy as an avowed European policy presupposes African subjection. The existence of white or black or brown or yellow supremacy implies the suppression, oppression, and exploitation of other people. You don't hear of English supremacy in England, French supremacy in France, or American supremacy in the U.S.A., because no Englishman intends dominating other Englishmen, no Frenchman intends dominating other Frenchmen, and no American intends dominating other Americans. But since the white man intends dominating Africa, he talks of white supremacy.'

Before we go into a somewhat detailed examination of European policies in Africa, we shall do well to note that, on the whole, white supremacy is the same thing as the Hebrew theory of 'a chosen people', and that it can only survive by presupposing the sub-humanity or human inferiority of other human beings. It has to do this to boost the ego, the pride of its own adherents. I am sometimes inclined to think that the day white supremacy is done away with in Africa, it will be much easier for genuine friendship to develop between Africa and the West.

What is the relation between white supremacy and the emergence of African nationalism? If we are to see what is really involved in this case, let us bear in mind throughout this chapter that white supremacy has produced two groups of people in Africa —the dominator and the dominated. It has divided Africa into two hostile camps. Those who dominate tend to hate those who resist domination, and those who are dominated tend to hate those who dominate. The struggle therefore is not one between black and white, but rather a natural struggle between the dominator and the dominated. What is involved is not whiteness or blackness, but the determined desire to dominate and the equally determined desire to throw off the yoke of domination. From the European camp we hear the voice of determination, 'We want to dominate all Africans'. And from the African camp we hear the thunderous reply, 'We don't want to be dominated by anybody', and so the tug-of-war goes on throughout the length and breadth of Africa.

But to do the fullest justice to the facts of the case, it is well for us now to go into the various European policies. We shall not overburden the reader with a detailed examination of these policies, but we shall only state fairly the spirit of these policies, for, indeed, it is not so much the structure of the policy that we want to understand as it is the spirit, motive, aim, goal, and purpose of that policy. The clash between black and white in Africa is one of motive, aim, goal, and purpose. It is a clash of interests, and one of the urgent problems in Africa today is how to reconcile European interests to those of Africans, and those of Africans to those of Europeans. Viewing it theologically, we may state the problem thus: How to teach the white man to live with his African neighbour, and how to teach the African to live with his white neighbour. In a nutshell: How to get black and white to accept each other.

We propose to begin our survey with Portuguese Africa, that is Mozambique and Angola. The Portuguese policy is based on the *assimilado* or *civilizado* system. According to this system an African who satisfies certain Portuguese official standards may become assimilated into Portuguese society and virtually become a white Portuguese except in colour, and enjoy those rights that are enjoyed by white Portuguese citizens. This is to say, an African can never become a full citizen in Portuguese Africa until he first becomes Portuguese. The whole aim of the Portuguese policy is to deal African nationalism a death-blow in its embryonic state. Nay, it is aimed at preventing the very conception of African nationalism. The African is taught, under the *assimilado* system, to think of himself as a Portuguese in Portugal, not as an African. The Portuguese policy aims at killing the African in the African and at replacing him with a Portuguese. A black-skinned Portuguese seems to be the goal of the Portuguese policy.

But the problem arises: the African wants to be himself. He does not want to lose his identity. He wants to be a citizen of his country without becoming a poor imitation of the Portuguese. An African from Lourenço Marques, Portuguese East Africa, stated his case well when he said, 'The Portuguese think that it was a mistake on the part of God to make the African African. Their *assimilado* policy is an effort to correct this divine error. However, people like to be themselves and to be accepted as such.'

But when I pointed out to him that the Portuguese policy of acceptance was better than that of non-acceptance, as existed in the Union of South Africa, he looked at me rather cynically and with an apparent surprise.

'No,' said he, 'there's no such thing as accepting the African. In Portuguese Africa today there are 11,000,000 who are neither citizens of Portugal nor of Africa.'

'But there are several thousands of Africans who have been assimilated and accepted', I said.

He laughed scornfully, and then said, as though he was talking to some poor ignorant boy hardly twelve years in this world, 'No, my boy. In accepting the several thousands of Africans as you say the Portuguese have done, the Portuguese are making it appear as though they are accepting the African, when all along they are staunchly refusing to accept the African.'

'I don't see that', I said.

'Well,' he said, 'in accepting the assimilated African, the Portuguese are merely receiving back their own Portuguese they pumped into him. In other words, they are really accepting themselves and not the African.'

I had never thought of it that way before. I mused over this refreshing thought, and my friend continued, 'You see, it's like saying, "Mr. White man, you are white and I am black. I shall have to paint you black before I can accept you." This would not be accepting the white man, but my black colour. It's the same thing with us.'

The idea of painting the white man black rather tickled me, though his logic impressed me. But my friend was in earnest, and he, perhaps thinking that I had not seen what he was trying to make me see, asked me, 'Do you know why you accept your own baby?'

'Well, that's my baby, and I'm its father', I said.

'But suppose you were sure that the baby to whom your wife gave birth was not yours, would you accept the baby?'

'That would be difficult', I said.

'Even though the baby came from your wife?' he asked.

'But the question is not whether it comes from my wife, but from me. And I suppose this holds true for my wife too. If I had a baby by another woman, the baby would not be acceptable to her either', I said.

'Quite right', he said eagerly. 'In other words, the baby has got to come from both of you to be acceptable to both of you.'

'Yes', I said.

'In other words, both of you do not accept the baby because it is a baby. You accept it because it is part of your flesh and bone.'

'I suppose so', I said.

'You see what the Portuguese are doing? They are impregnating the African with their Portuguese, and when the African gives birth to the Portuguese, they accept the Portuguese, not the African. They receive back what they put into the African. The *assimilado* system is a Portuguese refusal to accept the African as he is.'

This argument became more meaningful to me when I remembered that in Southern Rhodesia men and women of African descent receive the lowest pay, and those of mixed European and African descent receive higher pay, and those of European descent receive the highest pay in the country. The analogy was this, that the Government of Southern Rhodesia, which is almost exclusively white, does not see itself in the pure African and therefore legislates lower pay for Africans. But it is able to see itself more in Euro-Africans and therefore legislates higher pay for this group. The theory that seems to be established by this practice is, 'The nearer to the white skin, the better the treatment. The farther away, the worse the treatment.'

The core of Portuguese policy is perpetual political domination of the African, that is, perpetual subjection of the African so that the African may never come back to his own.

Closely related to the Portuguese *assimilado* system is the French policy of assimilation. When the *indigène* becomes civilized and cultured, he becomes a Frenchman and therefore acceptable to the French society, and full rights of citizenship are extended to him. This system is an attempt to absorb gradually educated Africans, and to include them in the central government of the state. This is quite a realistic policy on the part of the French since it would be bad politics to exclude Africans from all participation in the administration of the country.

But the French system of assimilation has glaring defects since it holds the Frenchman or French culture to be the ultimate goal for the African. It creates the false impression upon many African minds that there is nothing higher than to be a Frenchman, and many an African now resents having to direct all his efforts to becoming a Frenchman some day. The peoples of the world now live in glass houses and their very intimate weaknesses and moral frailties are on public view. The age of subtle pretensions has had its day. The Frenchman can no longer successfully pretend to the

African that he is the paragon of excellence. The African is now turning away from his French-aroused desire to become a Frenchman. He wants to remain African and enjoy life to its fullest without being deprived of his rights and privileges on the pretext that he does not look and behave like a Frenchman. It seems to be true all over Africa that the deluded African self that has been on a wild-goose chase—becoming Portuguese or French —is returning to its old self. African consciousness, which had been pushed into the background by the advent of European powers since the scramble for Africa in the nineteenth century, is now coming to the fore irresistibly. This new fact of African consciousness as a people renders the French system of assimilation anachronistic.

It is obvious that the French policy, like that of the Portuguese, is inherently one of political domination, and African nationalism in French Africa is the desire to overthrow this domination. The political struggles in French North Africa that resulted in the liberation and full independence of Tunisia and Morocco, and the present (1957) Algerian revolt against France, are good examples that show that the French system of assimilation has lost its once powerful grip over the French colonial peoples. The Moors and Arabs do not want to be French any more than a Frenchman wants to be a Moor or an Arab. The same spirit is spreading in French West Africa and French Equatorial Africa.

So much for the French policy. Let us now turn to the Belgian Congo—the home of about 13,000,000 blacks and 80,000 whites. This country, supplying 50 per cent of the world's uranium and 70 per cent of its industrial diamonds, is ruled directly from Brussels, so that both black and white have no franchise to speak of. There are no politics in the ordinary sense of the word, although John Gunther notes that there are 3,800 political prisoners.[1]

When an African in the Belgian Congo becomes westernized, he receives special credentials so that he can enjoy some of the legal rights enjoyed by the Belgian whites. In effect the spirit of the Belgian system of *évolués* or *immatriculés* is the same as that

[1] Gunther: *Inside Africa* (Harper, New York), p. 666.

of the Portuguese and French administrations—namely, indefinite political domination. The official Belgian policy is well stated in this sentence, 'We dominate to serve'.[1]

But the Belgian Africans resent this procedure of being labelled like commodities. An African observer from Southern Rhodesia expressed the attitude of the Belgian *évolué* thus: '. . . some educated self-respecting Africans refuse to qualify as *évolués*, because they regard it as being offensive to their human dignity.'[2] Their natural tendency is to regard themselves as Africans and not as Westerners.

The Belgian policy that equates domination with service has been satirized by several Africans who chaff in this strain: 'Imagine a man saying he's going to be the head of your village to serve you.' 'Imagine the U.S.A. descending upon Belgium and declaring "We'll dominate to serve you".' 'Imagine Russia going to Britain and offering the Belgian domination-service proposition. It's an immoral policy that, and like all immoral things it must come to a sad ending.'

Now let us turn to the policy of the Union of South Africa, and the word apartheid looms large in our minds. Apartheid is an Afrikaner word meaning apartness or separateness. As a political instrument it means social, economic, political, and sexual segregation on the basis of race. It is an effort to isolate from one another the white and the black races. But since geographical separation is not feasible, the apartheid policy, in actual practice, becomes one of both isolation and association. For practical reasons whites associate with blacks, but for purposes of dominating the African, they isolate themselves, by law, from the Africans. Prime Minister Strijdom's[3] slogan is *baasskap*— white supremacy. He has plainly stated, 'The white man will only succeed in remaining in South Africa if there is discrimination, in other words, only if we retain all power in our hands'.[4]

It would not be unfair to say (and we shall have occasion to elaborate on the point) that the whole spirit of the apartheid

[1] T. W. Wallbank: *Contemporary Africa*, p. 93.
[2] *The African Parade*, February 1957, p. 22.
[3] Mr. Strijdom died in 1958.
[4] T. W. Wallbank: *Contemporary Africa*, p. 86.

policy is to hold down the African, make him the worshipper of the white man, and to keep him as the drawer of water and hewer of wood for the white man. It is, in all seriousness, an 'underdog-making' policy, and the most objectionable expression of white supremacy.

We now turn to British Africa. Britain is the last European power whose policy we shall consider in this chapter. The British policy assumes various forms in different parts of British Africa. After the British government had experienced strong revolts in North America their policy of close control over the colonies changed to one of granting self-government to the colonies. The British policy in British Africa, as well as elsewhere, is one of training the Africans for eventual self-government within the Commonwealth of Nations. In place of an exclusive policy that created only a white government, the tendency of the British now is to have an inclusive policy so that the central government of the country reflects the different races living in that country. This type of government is called multiracial. The evolution of this form of government has remedied, up to a point, some of the glaring anomalies in British African administration.

The British policy, though in theory looking toward eventual self-government of the British colonies, in actual practice boils down to one of, 'Hold on as long as you can'. Of course, this is understandable when it is remembered that the British are not in Africa primarily for the good of Africa. It is evident, therefore, that their paper policy of eventual self-government for the colonies implies self-liquidation, which is by no means an easy thing to do as this is diametrically opposed to their interests. The main business of the British in Africa, in terms of their policy of eventual self-government, is to liquidate themselves, and it is only a perfect angel who can liquidate himself as quickly as possible for the benefit of those he dominates. If liquidation is inevitable, ordinary mortals try to liquidate themselves as slowly as they can. In short, no one liquidates himself willingly, and this is why it is that nearly every country that has received full independence from Britain has experienced a period of arrests and widespread imprisonment. It is a standing joke that 'when the British start arresting, full independence is around the corner'.

Be this as it may, the British policy is the best of all European policies in Africa in that it is realistic enough to accept the inevitable result that the country must eventually revert to its rightful owners. Although in many parts of British Africa the Africans are socially, economically and educationally discriminated against, nevertheless they enjoy direct representation, though out of proportion to their overwhelming numbers. The British policy, like other European policies we have discussed, subscribes to the doctrine of white supremacy, not only in theory, but also in practice.

We have now taken a bird's-eye view of the European policies in Africa, and our next task is to pick up the threads of our story and put them together in a meaningful whole so that we may see clearly the logical connexion between white supremacy and the upsurging African nationalism.

The overall European policy in Africa may be summed up in two words—white supremacy, and this is what the African means when he says, 'White people, from Cape to Cairo, are the same'. That is, they have a mania to rule Africa. This European policy is a great challenge to Africa, and since it is the nature of human existence to respond to challenge, the African peoples, despite their great geographical, linguistical, and ethnical differences, have been united by this challenge to which they are now responding positively and persistently. The law of 'the greater the challenge, the greater the stimulus' is in full operation on the continent of Africa. So long as the challenge remains, it would seem that the African peoples will continue, by every conceivable effort, to devise ways and means of overthrowing white domination without necessarily driving the white man out of Africa. The chances are that the white man, because he is too proud and too greedy to share life on an equal basis with the African, may leave Africa if equality of races becomes an accomplished fact.

If European policy had adopted, right from the beginning, an inclusive rather than an exclusive policy, it seems reasonable to surmise that African nationalism, as it is today, would have

36

been almost unknown. This is pure speculation and we do not pretend to know what would have happened if an inclusive policy had been followed; so that here we shall speak in terms of possibilities rather than of actualities.

On examination, the basic ingredients that go to make up the present African nationalism may be enumerated as the African's desire to participate fully in the central government of the country; his desire for economic justice that recognizes fully the principle of 'equal pay for equal work' regardless of the colour of the skin; his desire to have full political rights in his own country; his dislike of being treated as a stranger in the land of his birth; his dislike of being treated as means for the white man's end; and his dislike of the laws of the country that prescribe for him a permanent position of inferiority as a human being. It is this exclusive policy of white supremacy that has created a deep dissatisfaction among the African peoples. It is this exclusive policy that has brought to the fore the African's consciousness of kind. It seems reasonable to say that the present African nationalism is, paradoxically, the child of white supremacy, the product of an exclusive policy.

The question arises: since this exclusive policy has been largely responsible for the emergence of African nationalism, what European policy would have done a better job? We suggest seriously that an inclusive policy would have done it. By definition an inclusive policy takes in all those who come under its purview, and this is its chief merit since it does not ignore the needs of one section of the population in favour of the other. An exclusive policy, by its very nature, implies a disregard of one section of the people in favour of the other, and this is the real fatal weakness of white supremacy. A government that is orientated towards white supremacy fails miserably to serve the basic interests of a multiracial society. Those whose interests are deliberately ignored become dissatisfied and seek a government that has a truly inclusive view of the affairs of the country.

But even if we accept that an inclusive European policy would have done a much better job than the present exclusive European policy, the very fact that the policy is described as European

37

implies that it is external and foreign, and is exclusive in its actual essence, since Africa is multiracial. An inclusive policy forged in Africa on the anvil of true equal footing of all those races living in Africa, would be, in the main, acceptable to all.

To conclude our survey, we may now say that white supremacy is a stubborn rejection of the African by the white man, and that African nationalism is a reaction to that rejection. The African does not so much resent rejection in foreign countries, but he loathes it in the land of his birth. He wants to feel accepted by his fellow-men as man, and white supremacy is standing in his way, and he is determined to brush it aside. African nationalism is a struggle against white supremacy, and this struggle will continue to go on until white supremacy in Africa has given way to sound common sense—namely, that people, regardless of their colour or race, do not like to be treated as unwanted strangers in the land of their birth. The victory of African nationalism will therefore be the triumph of human personality and dignity.

CHAPTER FOUR

White Supremacy in Action

In a sense this chapter is an extension, or elaboration, of the preceding one, and yet, viewed from another angle, it merits separate treatment since here our main concern is to trace white supremacy in action, and not so much as an ideology. We want to see how this doctrine affects Africans in their daily life, and to do this we shall follow it in the major departments of human activity.

First, we shall endeavour to see how this European doctrine is carried out in the sphere of economic life. White people, like people of other races, equate economic power with political power. He who is economically powerful must, of necessity, be also politically strong. As the European ideology of white supremacy is to keep the African politically weak, it follows logically that one of the most effective ways of keeping him in that position is also to keep him economically weak. This is a round-about way of saying European political domination presupposes economic exploitation.

In most European-ruled African countries the principle of equal pay for equal work applies only in cases where a single race is involved. In exclusively white occupations this principle is accepted without question. Similarly, in predominantly African jobs the same procedure is followed. This is also true of Asiatic jobs. But in multiracial occupations it is accepted by neither government nor industry. Men of different races may hold the same positions, possess the same qualifications, and be equally efficient, but their economic reward is not determined according to their merit, but according to the colour of their skins. The highest economic benefit accrues to the white man, and the lowest to the African. The Asiatic and the coloured (mixed marriage) fall in between.

In industry the African is, also, barred from skilled and remunerative jobs. The white people resent economic equality just as they resent political equality with the African, and they will do anything to see that a state of inequality is maintained between whites and blacks. If they achieved this by equitable means, namely, efficiency, no reasonable African would quarrel with them. What hurts the African is that this is often achieved by foul play respectfully called discriminatory legislation. In the main, all skilled and highly remunerative jobs are reserved exclusively for white people. The efficient African is legally excluded from these so that his earning capacity is kept as low as possible for the preservation of white supremacy.

Land distribution in many European-ruled African countries is a very thorny question. In the Union of South Africa only 13·7 per cent of the land belongs to the Africans who form about 64 per cent of the total population; in Southern Rhodesia the African people own less than one-third of the land, and it is interesting to note that there are more than 2,000,000 Africans as against 180,000 white people. In Kenya the story more or less follows the same pattern. Even prejudiced experts on the causes of the Mau Mau movement admit that land of which the Kikuyu tribesmen had been deprived was among the major causes of the Mau Mau revolt. The general trend of land distribution in European-owned Africa has been to concentrate large African populations in small areas, and we shall return a little later to the effects of this. The second point to note is that the choicest parts of the land are often reserved for European owner-ship, and the worst parts for African acquisition.

Now let us turn to the meaning of these trends of land distribution so as to show the vicious circle they constitute. Since Africans are concentrated in small areas, human over-population becomes common. There is, in many parts of European-ruled Africa, over-population in sparsely populated areas! This surplus population in African areas has to move somewhere where there is more room, and so they drift from native areas to European areas; and since Europeans and the government own more land than they need, and more than they can actually use, they relieve this surplus population on their own economic terms. The result is a floating African population between native and European areas. This arrangement, though unsatisfactory to the African, is highly satisfactory for the European farmer who gets a cheap labour force resident on his land.

Phyllis Ntantala says, with regard to the South African situation:

'If we compare the rural land area with the rural population, we find that 124,186,000 morgen of land are owned and occupied by only 700,000 whites, while 6,025,547 Africans are crowded into 17,518,977 morgen of crown land called the "Native Reserves". The problem of the African, the cause behind this story of a people's agony, is LANDLESSNESS: LANDLESSNESS, so that the people will be forced out into the labour market, to the mines and farms where they will be herded together in camps, compounds and locations, where each white industrialist, farmer and housewife will be allotted his or her fair share of hands. In the towns only their labour is wanted—themselves not!'[1]

Closely connected with this human over-population is cattle over-population. Overstocking becomes a real problem, and what does the government do about this? It passes a law limiting the number of cattle an African may own, and if the African refuses to act in accordance with the law, the law deals with him accordingly. Of course, the white government does all this in the name of preventing soil erosion, conserving soil and water and flora! The sore point among many Africans, however, is that they may never increase their livestock since a natural increase, legally viewed, becomes overstocking and therefore an offence which can only be made good by disposing of that increase.

We can repeat what we have said so far by looking at the same thing in this way. In industry and commerce the white government says, 'Europeans better and bigger land; Africans poorer and smaller land'. In pastoral farming, 'Europeans more livestock and Africans less'. The whole economic structure in European-ruled Africa cripples the African's earning capacity, depreciating his economic value and keeping it as low as possible and so maintaining white supremacy. To the average white man

[1] Article, 'African Tragedy', appearing in *Africa South*, vol. 1, no. 3, April–June 1957, p. 67.

in Africa, economic equality is the same thing as political strangulation.

White supremacy exerts the same pressure in the political sphere. In Southern Rhodesia the African has the franchise. This franchise is based on qualification regardless of race. If a man is able to meet certain specific economic, educational, age, and residential qualifications he may register as a voter. But while the African in Southern Rhodesia enjoys this political right, yet to qualify for voting is very often a difficult matter since the economy of the country is built on a racial basis so that the African, who receives the lowest pay, finds it almost impossible to qualify. This is, incidentally, a good example of the interplay between economics and politics. The political rights are there for everyone without racial discrimination, but the means of qualifying for these rights are fully provided for whites only. These high political rights can only be reached by a long economic ladder. The white government makes the economic ladder of the white people as long as possible so that the majority can reach these rights, but the same government makes the economic ladder for the Africans as short as possible so that the majority of the Africans may never reach the same rights. It is an unfair handicap match from start to finish.

This point was clearly brought out when the British Colonial Secretary, Mr. Alan Lennox-Boyd, visited the Federation of Rhodesia and Nyasaland and was told by Mr. Harry Nkumbula (President of the Northern Rhodesian African Congress) and his followers in a special session that, 'Federation is a deliberate sabotage of the African's hopes for self-government and independence within the British Commonwealth of Nations. . . . Federation was created to place both economic and political power in the hands of the European minorities.'[1]

In the Federation of Rhodesia and Nyasaland the principle of direct representation by Africans has been accepted and fully implemented. There are twelve African members of parliament in the present (1959) Federal Assembly of Rhodesia and Nyasaland. These, in compliance with the constitutional provision of the

[1] *Christian Science Monitor*, 4 April 1957.

Federation, are reinforced by six specially elected European members of parliament who represent African interests in the House. The acceptance of direct African representation in parliament is, undoubtedly, a big advance on anything that obtains in the Union of South Africa, although candidness will not allow us to close our eyes to the anomalous situation that exists in the Federation—namely, that in a Federal Assembly of 59 members, 18 represent about 7,000,000 Africans, and the rest, that is, 41 members, represent only about 220,000 whites! The principle of deciding issues by majority gives way to that of white supremacy, and this phenomenon is repeated all over European-ruled Africa.

In British East Africa, that is Uganda, Kenya, and Tanganyika, the white political powers-that-be have now recognized that to have a government that is exclusively white in a multiracial country is as dangerous as it is illogical, and so a new multiracial form of government has been evolved. In Tanganyika, for example, since there are three major racial groups, a 10-10-10 system in the legislative council has been adopted. This is to say, 10 Europeans represent about 20,000 white people, 10 Africans about 7,000,000 Africans, and 10 Asians about 75,000 Asians.

In Kenya, where there is a population of about 6,000,000 Africans and about 44,000 whites, the composition of the multiracial government is less satisfactory. There are only 10 African representatives on a Legislative Council of 60 members.

We have quoted these concrete examples to illustrate that white supremacy is responsible for these legislative inconsistencies which now begin to stare the African in the face. There is a very strong desire, on the part of many whites, to bypass altogether the creation of a common electorate.

But of course these anomalies must not be taken to mean that British policy is the worst in Africa. Far from it. We have already indicated that it is the best of all European policies, though this is not to say it should continue as it is. We have already noted that it is only in British-controlled Africa that the African has a certain measure of franchise. In Portuguese Africa and the Belgian Congo the African enjoys no political rights. Even in French

Africa where the African may become a French citizen after assimilation, the African exercises his vote not so much in French Africa as in France, whereas in British Africa the African who has a vote exercises it in the African country concerned. We shall discuss more fully in the last chapter what steps are being taken to improve this situation between the black and white races of Africa. At the moment we merely seek to understand how white supremacy affects the African people.

If one visited the Union of South Africa, Southern Rhodesia, and Kenya, one would be greeted by a widespread display of such signs as NO AFRICANS ALLOWED, FOR EUROPEANS ONLY, on public parks, entrances, buses, railway stations, and other public places. These signs look cold and harmless, but they generate white heat in the African. Perhaps this might help the reader to feel vicariously what the African feels in the face of these signposts that daily humiliate him, and to assist the reader we suggest the following exercise:

Let an American visit any European city, and everywhere find signposts reading, NO AMERICAN ALLOWED. If on European trains, buses, public parks, railroad stations, post offices, and other public buildings the NO AMERICAN ALLOWED sign is prominently displayed so that it greets him at every turn and stop, and if that American's ire is not aroused, he could not be said to be normal. Let any Briton from Britain visit any of the independent African states, say, Ethiopia, Sudan, and Ghana, and be greeted with NO BRITON ALLOWED signs at every turn and stop, and he will feel very sharply that Britons are hated and unwanted in those states. Imagine what it feels like to an African when he is greeted by NO AFRICAN ALLOWED in the land of his birth. It is bad enough to be treated like this in foreign countries, but it is worse in one's own country.

There are many cases of social discrimination based on white supremacy which we should like to describe here. These are based on personal observation extending over thirty years in European-controlled Africa, but we cannot document these cases, and, since we are anxious not to give the wrong impression that we are here engaged in a piece of ingenious imaginative composition, we shall have to quote from elsewhere so that the reader may see how white supremacy affects the daily life of the African people in European-ruled Africa.

John Gunther is impartial and an authority with an unusually keen insight into the many problems confronting twentieth-century Africa. He writes:

'In some respects segregation is more pronounced in the Rhodesias than anywhere else in Africa, even Kenya and the Union [of South Africa] . . . racial discriminations in Rhodesia are among the most barbarous, shameful, and disgusting in the world.

'In Lusaka [Northern Rhodesia] when we were there Africans were not allowed in most European shops, but had to use hatchways. They stood in line out in the dust or rain in dark passageways on the side of or behind the shop, where a kind of peephole with a small ledge was built into the wall. Through this hatch they called out their wants, and merchandise was (if the white salesman inside chose to pay attention) pushed out to them through the slot. Africans were not allowed to touch or handle articles; they could not feel the texture of a bit of cloth or try on things, and they had no opportunity for looking around or making any choice.'[1]

Enough has been said about the social colour bar as a practical expression of white supremacy, and we shall not bother the reader with more quotations. We now turn to African education in European-ruled Africa. Here again, our intention is to demonstrate clearly that white supremacy like a lion roars, and roams the field of African education quite unconcerned with the full claims of educational justice for the African people. Throughout all European-ruled Africa, there is no compulsory African education. The intriguing question arises: why is there no compulsory education for African children?

At the very outset, let it be noted that African education is a political issue throughout European-ruled Africa. European powers administering the various parts of Africa have to keep on asking themselves this question: how far shall educational

[1] *Inside Africa*, pp. 632-3.

facilities be extended to the African people without upsetting the balance of the white man's control over Africa? The white man has enough decency to admit that education is good for the African too, but he has equally enough political cunning (not wisdom) to realize that universal education for Africans means the winding-up of the white man's rule in Africa. So he strikes a middle course, and he creates educational opportunity for a respectable minority while the majority have to do without schooling. Since he controls the politics and the economy of the country he finds this quite an easy task to perform. The reason he gives for lack of universal education for Africans is that there is no money in the state coffers, and there rests the matter! But there is always money for universal education for European children! When asked to account for this discrepancy, the answer usually given is, 'Too many African children'.

It is an impressive fact that South Africa, which produces 45 per cent of the world's gold and big quantities of mineral and agricultural products, cannot afford universal education for Africans; that the Belgian Congo with an output of 50 per cent of the world's uranium, 70 per cent of its industrial diamonds— let alone substantial quantities of copper, zinc, gold, manganese and annual production of £14,000,000 worth of cotton, £11,000,000 worth of coffee, and £10,000,000 worth of palm oil—cannot afford universal education for Africans!

In Tanganyika a European child costs the government annually £223 for his education, the African costs only £8 5s., and the Asian child £31! In French Equatorial Africa it is estimated that out of an African population of more than 4,000,000 only 20 per cent of the African children go to school although many more would go if there were more schools. Such facts as these could be quoted for other European-ruled African countries, but enough has been said to indicate our line of thought here.

Before we leave this aspect of our discussion, however, let us account again for the anomaly—Europeans, universal education; Africans, no universal education. Why these two different lines of approach? Perhaps some of the declared policies of some European powers will give us the answer.

J. G. Strijdom, the late Prime Minister of the Union of South Africa, said in 1953:

'Our policy is that the Europeans must stand their ground and must remain Baas [master] in South Africa. If we reject the Herrenvolk idea and the principle that the white man cannot remain Baas, if the franchise is to be extended to the non-Europeans, and if the non-Europeans are given representation and the vote and the non-Europeans are developed on the same basis as the Europeans, how can the European remain Baas? Our view is that in every sphere the European must retain the right to rule the country and to keep it white man's country.'[1]

This strong desire, among Europeans, to rule Africa also reflects itself in the lack of universal African education. Various European powers administering different parts of Africa may not express themselves so strongly as Strijdom, but they feel the same way. Hence the two different educational policies in the same European-ruled country.

African people now see how they are being subtly held down by this deliberate lack of universal education. There is, obviously, a relation between this realization and the emergence of African nationalism. John Gunther reports Awolowo of Nigeria as saying, in an interview, that the British did not have the true interest of the country at heart. 'In fourteen months, under the present government [Nigerian] we have done more for Nigeria than the British did in 120 years.'[2]

While we cannot swallow this hook, line and sinker, yet there is a great deal of truth in saying that the maximum benefit can never accrue to any country that is run primarily for the benefit of another country. India has the same story to tell that since she got her full independence there has been more rapid progress in the country. According to the Reverend Devapiriam A. Gregory of the Church of South India, Madura, 'When our people [Indians] got their independence they began working feverishly to improve their country. They felt it was theirs. They were working for their own benefit, not for the benefit of

[1] Quoted from Gunther: *Inside Africa*, p. 481.
Inside Africa, p. 775.

47

the British. India's independence has given our people new initiative. Little wonder that within ten years' time we [Indians] have done for our country more than the British did in 150 years.'

It is not our intention here to discredit Britain. We fully recognize that in many ways Britain laid the foundation for the progress that India is making during her maiden period of full nationhood. We merely quote this case to demonstrate that any given colonial power tends to look after her own interests first, and tends to neglect the legitimate needs of the natives of the country.

We are here trying to say that there is a great sense of urgency among Africans, a wave of realization sweeping throughout the entire continent that the African people are being purposely held back educationally, economically, and politically. There is a great desire to put matters right. This new desire has added more vitality to the African scene. This vitality must be diverted into the right channels for the good of all races who live in Africa.

Up to this point we have not touched directly on the important matter of human relations although we have done so in an indirect manner. We have already seen how the African is being economically retarded, politically discriminated against, socially rejected, stigmatized and humiliated, educationally neglected and deliberately held back. Our next consideration is: how far is the humanity of the African being affected by these adverse measures?

Before we answer this question, we wish to say that economic undervaluing, political domination, social segregation, and educational neglect of any given people, be they black, or white, or yellow, or brown, have a corresponding effect of degrading the human status of such people. You cannot effect a racially discriminatory economic downgrading of any given people without a corresponding downgrading of their humanity. You cannot have political domination of any one race by another without the former dehumanizing the latter. Domination by one race in any multiracial society tends to relegate the other races to inferior, if not sub-human, status. The life of those so dominated becomes almost worthless compared to that of those who dominate as a racial group.

We have now arrived at another angle of vision in our discussion on the emergence of African nationalism. It is that the African's firm stand against white supremacy is his practical expression against that which downgrades his humanity or human status. His desire for full independence is another way of trying to remove this European machinery of administration which is persistently telling him, 'You're not so much of a human being'. The elevation of African status is ultimately the elevation of human status. Those who champion the African cause champion that of humanity. (Incidentally, is the Freedom Radio to Communist-dominated Eastern Europe not a fight for human rights? Here the Eastern European situation interlocks with that of European-ruled Africa, the only difference being that Eastern Europe hopes to remove Russian domination, but Africa wants to remove European domination.)

We shall not press this point further until we come to the last chapter where we wish to sum up the results of our discussion, and give what we feel, in the light of our survey, to be a reasonable course of action. But for the time being let it suffice to state that in any multiracial society, where one race is legally held up as the object of worship by the other races, ordinary human justice becomes almost an impossible feat in matters involving those who dominate and those who are dominated. Rightly have some African preachers characterized white supremacy as 'the white man's Golden Calf, to which even Justice must bow in reverence'.

Alan Paton, who is very sensitive to the basic problems of the African people, says:

'One thing seems clear, that ultimately no political solution of the problem can endure unless it has the support of the politically unawakened and politically awaking African people. We [whites] would be foolish to expect that this support will be given to any solution which seems to them [Africans] to detract from their dignity as human beings. If I know or understand anything of the African people, it is that they have a fierce hunger to be recognized by the people of the world as their fellows and equals.'[1]

[1] *South Africa in Transition*, p. 70.

CHAPTER FIVE

The Christian Church

In the last two chapters we discussed at length white supremacy as one of the major factors in the rise of African nationalism. In this chapter we wish to survey the role the Christian Church has played in the forging of African nationalism on the anvil of history. We shall attempt to assess the influence the Christian Church has exercised on the minds, attitudes, and outlook of the African people who have had direct contact with it. The statistical method cannot be of much help here since it cannot help us to measure those subtle changes which become responsible for great things. Spiritual realities defy any mathematical manipulation, and for this reason we shall, in the course of our survey, single out outstanding events and individuals to exemplify in what ways the Christian Church has influenced the African people.

Let it be noted right from the outset that when the missionaries went to Africa, they had not the slightest idea of helping African nationalism as such. Their primary goal was to propagate the Gospel of Christ to their fellow human beings. The Church has been only a blind instrument in the whole process of African nationalism. On the whole, missionaries in Asia and Africa have been accused, and not without cause, of standing in the way of emerging nationalism. In the main, they have been staunch supporters of colonial rule so that colonial powers cannot blame the rise of African nationalism on the missionaries as a class. Our survey will, however, show that missionaries, unwittingly, have been equally helpful to the upsurging African nationalism.

To appreciate fully the part that the Christian Church has taken in the development of the gigantic continent of Africa, we shall do well to recapitulate, in a rather jet-like fashion, some of the basic historical facts about Africa before we attempt the task of determining the influence of the Christian Church on Africa.

Prior to the coming of the missionaries to Africa, there were only four out of more than 700 different languages that had a native script of their own. The four that had a written form were the Ethiopian Amharic, the Arabic, the Berber Tamachek, and the Liberian Vai. The other languages, though with highly developed grammar and syntax, were only oral. This is to say that, prior to the coming of the Christian Church, Africa was grossly cursed with illiteracy, and she still is, but to a lesser degree. But since the coming of the missionaries great strides have been made in the field of literacy. It is estimated that 10-12 per cent of the African population can now read and write with varying degrees of proficiency. African literacy is definitely on the increase. The demand for schools greatly exceeds the supply. There is everywhere in Africa an unprecedented hunger for education and literature. Even the uneducated African parents try to make sure that their children get the opportunity they themselves never had. They can sense the value of education for their children. Schools ranging from the dilapidated pole-and-mud hut to the most up-to-date school building are steadily increasing in the bush, farm, town, and city, but the pace is rather too slow for the feverish desire 'to get an education'.

While in American history it is common to talk of the Californian Gold Rush of 1849, there is such a thing as an African 'Education Rush' of the twentieth century. The Christian Church has introduced a new spirit of learning without which no nation can have a truly balanced progress. It is this creative spirit that helps to sustain African nationalism and without which the whole idea would end in dismal failure.

Since the coming of the missionaries to Africa the Holy Bible has been rendered into 33 African languages, the New Testament in 70, and between 200 and 300 of these languages have been reduced to writing. What is the actual relevance of the Bible or the New Testament to African nationalism? We need not elaborate to any great length that the Bible has most powerful ideas for the heart and for the mind. No man can be brought up on the Bible and remain uninfluenced by it. If it is true that the teachings of the Holy Bible greatly helped in the shaping of European thought, the same thing could be said of Africa. If it is true that the United States owes much to the Bible, the same thing could be said of Africa.

One of the unique teachings of the Bible, especially the New Testament, is the worth and dignity of the individual in the sight of God, and there is a relation between this teaching and the present African nationalism. According to African tradition, at least in some parts if not in the whole of Africa, the individual counted in so far as he was part and parcel of the group, outside of which he lost his real worth. In actual practice this meant that no individual could follow his natural bent beyond the group. All new schemes, new adventures, new thoughts, and new outlooks on life were subject to the approval or disapproval of the group. The individual, to all practical intent, was dominated by the fear of the group; let alone the fear that comes from ignorance, superstitious beliefs and belief in the existence of evil spirits. The individual, socially, spiritually, and mentally, moved in shackles, and this was certainly not conducive to progress. Individual initiative was crippled. But now the African individual is being delivered from these fetters. The individual is being invested with a new status, and so today we find individuals venturing beyond the confines of the group, and in many cases the group now looks upon this new individual as its real saviour. The Bible is redeeming the African individual from the power of superstition, individuality-crushing tradition, witchcraft, and other forces that do not make for progress. The same Bible is helping the African individual to reassert himself above colonial powers! It is inconceivable to a logical mind that the Bible could deliver the African from traditional domination without at the same time redeeming him from colonial domination. If the Bible teaches that the individual is unique, of infinite worth before God, colonialism, in many respects, says just the opposite; so that, in actual practice, Biblical teachings are at variance with colonialism, and it becomes only a matter of time before one ousts the other. The Bible-liberated African is now reasserting himself not only over tribal but also over colonial authority, since these two are fundamentally the same.

Two South African natives were arguing one day over the

unhealthy South African situation. One was inclined to censure the whole missionary enterprise in Africa in this strain, 'You see, the missionary came here and said, "Let us pray". And we closed our eyes. And when we responded "Amen" at the end of his prayer, we found the Bible in our hands. But lo! our land had gone!'

To which the other replied, 'When Europeans took our country we fought them with our spears, but they defeated us because they had better weapons. And so colonial power was set up much against our wish. But lo! the missionary came in time and laid explosives under colonialism. The Bible is now doing what we could not do with our spears.'

The present African nationalism is strongly undergirded by Christian principles. Gandhi, who was responsible for the liquidation of British imperialism in India, admitted, though himself a professed Hindu, that Christ's Sermon on the Mount had greatly influenced him. The Reverend Martin Luther King, leader of the Negro Bus Boycott in Montgomery, Alabama, U.S.A., says, in his article, 'Nonviolence and Racial Justice':

'The method of nonviolence is based on the conviction that the universe is on the side of justice. It is this deep faith in the future that causes the nonviolent resister to accept suffering without retaliation. He knows that in his struggle for justice he has cosmic companionship. This belief that God is on the side of truth and justice comes down to us from the long tradition of our Christian faith.'[1]

The above quotation, drawn from the American scene, becomes more enlightening when placed alongside the African scene. The South African 'treason' case, which placed 156 Africans, Europeans, and Asiatics under arrest, reveals the influence of the Christian principles on the South African situation. Mr. George Houser, in his article 'Treason in South Africa?', writes about those in jail:

'A rededication ceremony was conducted in the Fort [prison]. Chief Luthuli's brief speech closed with the Challenge: "If there are any present who are sorry to be in the Fort and regret that

[1] *Christian Century*, 6 February 1957.

their membership in [the African National] Congress has brought them to this pass, let them drop out of the circle. Only those of us who are determined to continue the struggle may sing *Mayibuye* [the freedom song, 'Let Africa Return']." Everyone sang. Chaplain Gawe led in prayer. The ceremony ended with the singing of the African National Anthem, *Nkosi Sikelela Afrika* —God Bless Africa.'[1]

But it is not only the African Christian who stands against those forces which deny him freedom. True European Christians are also on the side of the African, but perhaps this is to state the matter rather incorrectly since there is no particular virtue in being on the side of either the African or the European. It is more correct to say that true European Christians are standing on the side of that which is right—namely, that oppression or suppression of any human being is wrong. What goes on in colonial Africa shocks the Christian conscience of both black and white so that, in a real sense, white supremacy finds itself engaged in a life-and-death struggle with Christian principles. The Anglican Church of South Africa, for instance, has taken an uncompromising position on the apartheid policy. When the Nationalist Government of the Union of South Africa introduced the new Native Laws Amendment Bill (1957) which would bar interracial gatherings of any kind, the late Archbishop Clayton, in collaboration with four other Anglican bishops, wrote to the Prime Minister and stressed the official position of the Anglican Church, which is the second largest denomination in the country:

'The Church cannot recognize the right of an official of the secular Government to determine whether or where a member of the Church of any race (who is not serving a sentence which restricts his freedom of movement) shall discharge his religious duty of participation in public worship, or to give instructions to the minister of any congregation as to whom he shall admit to membership of the congregation.

'Further, the constitution of the Church of the Province of South Africa provides for the synodical government of the Church. In such synods, bishops, priests and laymen are repre-

[1] *Christian Century*, 6 March 1957.

sented without distinction of race or colour. Clause 29(c) makes the holding of such synods as dependent on the permission of the Minister of Native Affairs.'[1]

Bishop Vernon Inman of Natal, South Africa, says:

'As a Church we loathe and abominate the devilish device known as Apartheid and we believe it is leading our country to ultimate ruin. . . .

'We continue to oppose it as un-Christian and we emphasize that it is un-South African. . . .

'I imagine that not even a heathen would suppose that God would even tolerate Apartheid in his own house.'[2]

It is not only the Anglican Church that is battling against racial discrimination, but also such denominations as the Methodist, Roman Catholic, Congregational, and Salvation Army. This is not only true of South Africa, but of such countries as the Federation of Rhodesia and Nyasaland, British East Africa, and other African countries where Christian churches and Christian councils fight for ordinary human justice for the African.

We have had to quote at length in order to show that the Christian Church has created in Africa, at least in some parts of Africa, a strong Christian consciousness that transcends the usual barriers of race and colour, and this Christian consciousness is based on the love of God and the love of our fellow-men. It is based on a strong sense of human justice. The story of African nationalism would be incomplete if this Christian awareness was ignored since it is this awareness that is an integral part of the creativeness of African nationalism. The strength of this Christian consciousness was even demonstrated by the African Christians in Kenya who remained obdurate in the face of Mau Mau terrorism. They chose to suffer and die rather than repudiate their Christian principles which were much disliked by the Mau Mau terrorists.

Of course, the non-Christians also support this movement. But while African nationalism is strongly motivated by African consciousness of an oppressed people seeking freedom, it is

[1] *The Natal Mercury*, Durban, 9 March 1957.
[2] Ibid.

Christian consciousness that gives it the proper direction and that self-sustaining creativity which makes for human progress. The Christian faith may be regarded in one sense as its spiritual father, whether or not the Church recognizes that role. In another sense, the Church may be regarded as the guardian angel of African nationalism. Practically all important African political leaders went through the Christian Church school. The African politician may turn his nose up in derision, and twist his lips by way of deprecation, when he hears it said that the Christian Church laid secure political foundations for African nationalism, but that need not surprise us, for two reasons. First,

> But 'tis a common proof,
> That lowliness is young ambition's ladder,
> Whereto the climber-upward turns his face;
> But when he once attains the upmost round,
> He then unto the ladder turns his back,
> Looks in the clouds, scorning the base degrees
> By which he did ascend.[1]

And second, a few missionaries, working in a colonial atmosphere, also adopted a colonial attitude towards the African and stood between the latter and his big dream of independence. The few erring missionaries, however, should not be confused with the main stream of missionaries who, by example and precept, have demonstrated the reality of Christian principles. The fact is that the Christian faith is like a highly prolific fruit tree whose fruit gives life to those who care and to those who do not care for it. Christian and non-Christian Africans have reaped, in varying degrees, the blessings of the Christian faith, and this is as it should be since God himself sends rain on the just and the unjust.

We have said enough about the influence of Christianity upon the African—altogether about 22,000,000 Africans profess the Christian faith—and now we want to turn to the Christian schools that have played so important a part in the lives of the African people. But we must make one more observation before we turn our thoughts to African education. The Christian Church

[1] *Julius Caesar*, ii. i.

has replaced, in many parts of Africa, the otherwise exclusive clan or tribal worship to which only the members of the clan or tribe went. Members of different clans and tribes now worship together. There now exists among the different clans and tribes of Africa religious communication. The Church, in a real sense, has helped the religious unification of many parts of Africa, and this is evidenced, as we have already stated, by the existence of the Holy Bible in more than 33 African languages, of the New Testament in more than 70 languages, and of parts of the Bible in about 300 African languages. In many places tribal consciousness is being pushed into the background, and Christian consciousness is coming to the fore.

The average African educational curriculum includes, on the academic side, the European language that is spoken by the administering colonial power, one African language, religious instruction, arithmetic, history, geography, physical training, singing, physiology and hygiene, and nature study. On the practical side, it includes woodwork, vegetable gardening, poultry, animal husbandry, brickmaking, forestry, and general manual work. Girls do sewing, laundry, and housekeeping. On the recreational side, it includes athletic sports, soccer, basketball, volleyball, and baseball. The extracurriculum includes Girl Guides (Girl Scouts), Boy Scouts, debates, drama and variety shows.

After elementary education girls and boys may train as teachers. The teacher-training curriculum consists of child study, teaching methods, school organization, practical teaching, and other subjects incidental to the teaching profession. Boys and girls may also train as medical orderlies and nurses. In addition to these professional schools there are also trade schools where boys train as builders, carpenters, agricultural demonstrators, and forestrymen. In most cases these artisans turn out very good work by any standards.

What we have said so far suffices to indicate the nature and scope of the Church-related and government schools in the various parts of Africa. But we have not attempted to measure the actual influence of education on the African people, and we now propose to do that.

The study of European, English, and American, as well as African history in African schools, has had a profound influence upon the African people. The European struggle for liberty, for religious toleration, for freedom of thought and expression, and European resistance against tyranny, thrill the African students to the core. How often have my history students requested me to tell them about certain historical figures! 'Please, Sir, tell us about that tenacious English Bulldog [Sir Winston Churchill].' 'Please, Sir, tell us more about Martin Luther and his ninety-five theses. Oh, that man! He was a man!' 'Mahatma Gandhi whose soul was more powerful than the British Navy and Royal Air Force put together.' 'Tell us, please, about the Boston Tea Party.' 'David Livingstone the man who stopped the slave trade in Central Africa.' 'Please tell us about Mr. Government-of-the-People-by-the-People-and-for-the-People [Abraham Lincoln].' European, American, and Indian heroism thrills African students. They admire the firm stand against tyranny. But sooner or later the African admirer seeks to overthrow the tyranny of his European hero so long as the latter appears the dictator in relation to the former. Perhaps the following account will make our point clear.

Many historical incidents are being twisted to give them an African flavour. The famous American dictum, 'No taxation without representation', sometimes runs, 'No racial peace without African representation'. The American song, *John Brown's Body*, was, when Dr. Kwame Nkrumah was jailed by the then British administration, changed by the then Gold Coasters to:

Kwame Nkrumah's body lies amould'ring in the jail
But his soul goes marching out.

When the students' spokesman had finished presenting the students' grievances to the principal of one mission school in Southern Rhodesia, he stopped in the midst of a tense atmosphere of over 400 students, and bowed stiffly to the principal, and said by way of conclusion, 'Sir, we thought it was right and proper that this matter should be brought before you in this fashion so that government of the students, by the students, and for the students shall not perish from this Mission Station'.

Abraham Lincoln's Gettysburg address had been taught for the beauty of its prose which borders on poetic perfection; it had been taught to improve the students' oral English—the rising and falling inflection, clear enunciation and good choice of simple, powerful words; but alas, it had turned out to be a handy political weapon!

At this juncture, I am also reminded of the Rev. E. T. J. Nemapare of Southern Rhodesia who broke away from the Methodist Church in Southern Rhodesia and established an indigenous church of his own. He met with a storm of opposition from his Mother Church. He was seriously accused of 'breaking the body of Christ', and in his defence he stated, 'No Protestant has any right to accuse me of breaking the body of Christ. It is my Protestant right to protest, and I do not see what's wrong with exercising my birthright.' He remained unmoved and went ahead with his indigenous church. The Rev. Mr. Nemapare had been taught Church history during the course of his evangelistic training. The curriculum had been drawn up by the Church officials, but the application of the contents was entirely his own.

The African finds himself confronted by the European colonial powers. They stand over against him, and more so as he is relegated to a position of inferiority in the land of his birth. He wants to understand how the control of Africa slipped from the hands of its rightful owners, and to do this he likes to study European history even long after he has left school. And the next thing he does is to study how the control of Africa can be restored to its rightful owners, and so he studies movements of liberation—that is, movements of overthrowing an imposed rule, and so the Glorious English Revolution of 1688, the American Revolutionary War of 1776, the French Revolution of 1789, and the Russian Revolutions of 1917 occupy his attention. He wants to understand how other people got their independence so that he may also get his. He studies history with a practical end in view. He has problems to solve. He is not so much interested in pure as in applied knowledge. 'Other people did it. Why can't we?' he often asks himself after the lessons of history have thoroughly convinced him that he has much in common with the rest of the peoples of the world. The African Freedom Salute, *Mayibuye!*—Let Africa Return—points out clearly that Africans, in general, believe that Africa has gone away from them, and it also shows the African's strong belief that Africa will one day return to her rightful owners. The question that many an African is asking himself today is: How can we help Africa return to her rightful owners? And the study of history is giving the African many suggestions. It is not our concern here to state whether those suggestions are right or wrong. Our task, as we have already stated, is to examine those factors that are helping in the forward thrust of the African national movements.

Prime Minister Kwame Nkrumah's reading list may perhaps give more substance to what we have stated up to this point. Dr. Kwame Nkrumah says:

'I devoted much energy to the study of revolutionaries and their methods. Those who interested me most were Hannibal, Cromwell, Napoleon, Lenin, Mazzini, Gandhi, Mussolini, and Hitler. I found much of value to be gleaned and many ideas that were useful to me later in my own campaign against imperialism.

'At first I could not understand how Gandhi's philosophy of non-violence could possibly be effective. It seemed to me to be utterly feeble and without hope of success. The solution of the colonial problem, as I saw it at that time, lay in armed rebellion. How is it possible, I asked myself, for a revolution to succeed without arms or ammunition? After months of studying Gandhi's policy and watching its effect, I began to see that, when backed by a strong political organization, it could be the solution to the colonial problem. In Jawaharlal Nehru's rise to power I recognized the success of one who, pledged to socialism, was able to interpret Gandhi's philosophy in practical terms.'[1]

We can safely say then that the study of history has placed very powerful political weapons in the hands of many Africans, and that historical consciousness is one of the chief factors undergirding African nationalism. The educated African has very powerful ideas and ideologies that are highly explosive and dangerous to colonialism.

[1] *Ghana: The Autobiography of Kwame Nkrumah* (Nelson, Edinburgh), pp. xiii–xiv.

Now we turn to the study of European languages. This usually consists of reading, oral, grammar, dictation, spelling, essay-writing, letter-writing, comprehension exercises, and general European literature. On the Junior and Senior Cambridge, or matriculation level, as well as on the university level, African students follow exactly the same English syllabus as the one followed by English-speaking students. The examinations given are the same, and the diplomas awarded are also the same. The study of European languages has aroused such a keen interest among Africans that at times it borders on fanaticism. No African considers himself modern and well educated unless he has mastered some European language. There is nothing new in this. During the Hellenistic period those who could not speak the Greek language were deprecatingly called barbarians, not cultured. With the ascendancy of Rome, Latin became the learned man's language, and at a later date French became every cultured man's language. This European tendency has now spread over the entire continent of Africa. But, of course, this is no European tendency. The conquered tend to copy the language and customs of the conqueror. Just as many leading Indians have been brought up on English literature, many leading Africans in British Africa have also been brought up on the same English syllabus. This fact is also true of French and Portuguese Africa. Such African professional men as lawyers, teachers, doctors, journalists, parliamentarians, accountants, carry on their work in some European language common in Africa. And so, European languages are now understood and spoken in many parts of Africa, not only by the 5,000,000 Europeans there, but also by at least 40,000,000 Africans. In other words the Church school in Portuguese, British, and French Africa, has brought the European languages to the very doors of the African people.

We have already referred to the medley of African languages —over 700 of them. This has been held as one of the factors responsible for the countless divisions found all over Africa. The various tribal groups have been walled off from one another not only by geographical barriers, but also by language difficulties. Linguistically, an African from the Union of South Africa is as much of a foreigner to another from Kenya, as an English-speaking American would be to a Russian or German. Even Africans within the same country are linguistic foreigners to one another since one country may have more than one language. In Southern Rhodesia, for instance, there are two main native languages which make one section regard the other as foreigners. It is estimated that there are 250 different tribes in Nigeria, and that each tribe has its own language, but for practical purposes these are sometimes reduced to twenty. At present, it is common to talk of only three major languages of Nigeria, namely, Yoruba, Ibo, and Hausa. These groups are strictly according to the three major regions of the country. In Liberia there are about twenty native languages with a population of about 2,000,000 people. In South Africa there are five major native languages spoken by about 9,000,000 natives. This could be said of any other African country. An African observer once said, 'Language divisions have made the white man thrive very well in Africa. The day these close up, the white man will have to change his technique.'

One of the results of the study of European languages is the breakdown of these linguistic walls found all over Africa. I have met in the U.S.A. Africans from Ghana, Nigeria, Liberia, Sierra Leone, the Union of South Africa, Kenya, Tanganyika, Uganda, and Ethiopia, and but for the English language we learned at school we would have remained a closed secret to one another. As soon as we meet we feel quite at home with one another because we are able to communicate with one another. The traditional language barriers between us have been removed. One English-speaking African is perfectly at home with another English-speaking African from any part of Africa. The same thing is true of Portuguese-speaking and French-speaking Africans. The Africans are now able to convey their thoughts and ideas to one another on a much broader basis. A common language is very useful in the forming and shaping of the common destinies of peoples of diverse backgrounds. While we do not pretend that all Africans in British, French, and Portuguese Africa now speak English, French, and Portuguese respectively, we want to make it clear that while in African tribe A only 10 per cent may speak English, the same thing may be true of tribes B, C, D, E, F, G, and the like, so that communication through the medium of English is carried on among these literate members of A, B, C, D, E, F, and G, and the result is an exchange of ideas, thoughts, aspirations, plans and frustrations, and these are interpreted into the vernacular for the benefit of the illiterate masses, and thus even the illiterate become more enlightened by the study of European languages. The Africans say, 'You can learn the tricks of a man by learning his language'.

The Christian Church, by sending religious, educational and industrial missionaries to Africa has broadened the outlook of many an African; it has provided opportunities for many Africans to develop their latent qualities, and it has discouraged tribal hatred and encouraged universal brotherhood instead. In many ways the Christian Church has provided Africa with sound African political leadership. The present enlightened African political leadership would be next to impossible but for the Christian Church that spread literacy to many parts of Africa.

CHAPTER SIX

The Positive Role of Colonialism

Up to this point we have not directly credited colonialism as such with the emergence of African nationalism. An examination of the forces that are at work in the shaping of African nationalism would be incomplete if the positive role of colonialism was ignored altogether. We therefore propose to scrutinize the major areas wherein colonialism has brought real progress to the peoples of Africa. But, let this be understood from the beginning, we are not here pleading for the continuance or perpetuation of colonialism on the continent of Africa. We are merely seeking to understand the positive role of colonialism. We are fully aware that to most African people colonialism means the deprivation of their freedom by European powers.

As the scramble for Africa caused a great deal of confusion and unnecessary toe-treading among European powers, it became necessary that the spheres of influence, by different European powers having claims to Africa, be formally defined. With this aim in view Prince Bismarck, for the Imperial German Government, invited interested powers, and what is now known as the Berlin Conference of 1884 was duly convened. In 1885 this Conference came out with what is usually called the Berlin Act of 1885. Among other things stipulated in the Berlin Act were freedom of trade for all nations, suppression of the slave-trade, the civilizing of the natives of Africa as well as their evangelization, protection of religions, scientific and charitable institutions, and the preservation of law, order, and peace.[1]

This Act threw Africa open to more missionaries, explorers, traders, scientists, and new institutions since it guaranteed protection, good order, and peace. One of the blessings of the advent of European powers in Africa was the suppression of slavery and the slave-trade. The gigantic wave of humanitarianism that was sweeping across the whole continent of Europe coincided with

[1] T. W. Wallbank: *Contemporary Africa*, pp. 108–9.

European expansion to Africa. The abolition of slavery in Africa was the practical expression of this European humanitarianism. The Berlin Act did, among other things, two things—namely, it greatly stimulated European imperialism, and at the same time it encouraged the liquidation of that imperialism. Here, again, we come up against the paradox of history, and this is occasioned by the very provisions of the Berlin Act, which can be summarized thus—to acquire African land and to civilize the African. Land acquisition, in the course of events, turned out to be imperialism, and civilizing the African turned out to be the liquidation of that imperialism.

What did the European powers mean when they asserted that they wanted to civilize the native of Africa? Whatever the content of civilization is, in European terms, one thing remains clear: to civilize a primitive people means to bridge the gap between the civilized and the uncivilized. In other words, to bring the primitive man to the level of the civilized man. Stating the same thing differently, one would say that any programme of civilizing any given people tends to create a community of thoughts and ideas common to both the bearer of civilization and the newly initiated. This is to say that the process of civilizing a primitive people is one of liquidating the monopolistic position of those who dedicate themselves to civilizing others. The logical conclusion of the civilizer and the civilized becoming partners or equals is just as inescapable as that of the training of boys and girls who eventually become colleagues of their professors. If then the Berlin Conference was motivated purely by imperialistic designs in the opening-up of Africa, history has cheated the European powers in that the rise of African nationalism directly cuts across European imperialism. It should be remembered, as we have pointed out elsewhere, that in many ways European imperialism in Africa has given to African nationalism such strength as we have not known in African history. If, on the other hand, the Berlin Conference was motivated by a genuine spirit of civilizing the African natives, then the European Powers are achieving their main objectives in the rise of African nationalism since it is the desire of the African people to reach the same level as the European powers who set out to civilize them, or to use our phrase, to bridge the gap between them and the Africans.

But let us now return to our original discussion of the positive role of colonialism in Africa. With the passing away of the institution of slavery, the European-owned and African-owned slaves were accorded new human status. Let it be noted in passing, that the general outlook of a slave on life is different from that of a free man. His potential capacities are crippled, stunted, and pushed into the dim background. The emancipation of slaves therefore opened a new world to thousands upon thousands of African slaves. Hence, it can be rightly said that European colonial powers, by dealing slavery a severe death-blow, set the whole continent of Africa on a new venture of freedom and human dignity.

The advent of European powers in Africa not only saw slavery come to an end, but also the terrible tribal wars. What are now the Union of South Africa, Southern Rhodesia, Nigeria, Ghana, and Portuguese and French Africa were torn with count-less tribal wars, so that the chief occupation of most able-bodied African men was that of raiding other tribes. We are, of course, aware that Europe itself is a war-torn, war-cursed country. But be this as it may, it remains a fact beyond contention that European powers, as they had superior weapons to those of the Africans, were able to impose peace on the African people, and this has been to the general good of the continent of Africa. With this new freedom from tribal wars, men soon found something else to do. Something more creative took the place of destructive tribal wars. It is obvious, however, that with the European dictator of peace at the top, the African soon lost the control of his country, but gained peace and good order which made for real progress. The European powers, although they had failed to keep peace in Europe, were soon regarded by most native tribes as 'peace-makers', bearers of 'deeds of humanity', and 'bringers of enlightenment'. Indeed, it has been rightly asserted by both Africans and Europeans that European occupation of Africa, although it deprived people of their independence, helped to direct the minds and activities of the native peoples away from destructive to constructive programmes of action.

When European powers came to Africa, their immediate objects were trade, mining, and farming. They came strictly for business. As more European settlers came, more European villages, towns, and later cities, sprang up and towered above natural vegetation. Many mines for gold, diamonds, chrome, asbestos, copper, and uranium were opened, and to these thousands, and afterwards millions, of Africans flocked to work, or to have adventure. For the first time the African went into the bowels of the earth. There he drilled holes into the hard rock, and was an eyewitness to 'things that split rocks, and send pieces of rock flying into the air'. It was overpowering, overwhelming, and all-exciting. The novelty of it all continued for quite some time. 'Wonders have come', the Africans used to say again and again as they reflected on these new experiences. In the towns and cities many Africans were employed as domestic servants, factory workers, and general labourers. Many joined the police force. On the farm many saw new agricultural implements and entirely new methods of farming. Thousands of Africans were employed in the construction of roads, bridges, railroads, and dams. Many Africans began learning new Western skills so that today you get armies of Africans who drive taxis, trains, cranes, and tractors. African builders and carpenters have come to stay. There is, without doubt, a general wave of Westernization sweeping throughout the continent of Africa, and this has had, in general terms, beneficial effects on the people.

We could write volumes on the good things that European powers brought to Africa, but this lies outside the scope of this book. We want the reader to note these four things, among others, that the coming of European powers has brought to Africa: the coming together of different tribes, better communications, a new economic system, and the creation of new classes among the African people. We shall now deal with each of these.

With the coming of mines, towns, and cities the different tribes of Africa found themselves thrown together. Tribesmen who had never had anything to do with one another found themselves living together in one area, working side by side with one another, and the need to get along well with one another became imperative. For instance, in the Johannesburg gold-mines tribes from British East Africa, Portuguese Africa, British Central Africa, South West Africa, Basutoland, Swaziland, Natal, the Cape Province, and the Orange Free State are to be found in big numbers. Southern Rhodesia is full of native labourers from Northern Rhodesia, Nyasaland, Tanganyika, and other neighbouring territories. Briefly, colonialism introduced African tribes to one another. With the coming together of these tribes the horizons of many Africans have been greatly extended. While the U.S.A. is popularly regarded as the melting-pot of the nations, it is equally true that every mine, town, and city in Africa is a melting-pot of the tribes. Many Africans who have been thus urbanized have learned that what counts in the long run is not belonging to this or that tribe, but rather, to use the Ndebele phrase, to *sebenza nzima*—to work hard. Eventually the African regarded himself not so much as a tribesman, but as a worker. A common language—a kind of lingua franca—soon developed, and thus communication was facilitated among members of different tribes. Down in the mine, in factories, the police force, domestic service, on the farm, in the store, hospital, clinic, and a host of other European-introduced institutions and occupations, no tribal barriers existed or were encouraged. People just mixed freely. To say the least, tribalism is on its way out, and something else is taking its place. It is estimated that over 40,000,000 Africans have left the tribal regime and have been caught up in the industrial system. In the Belgian Congo it is estimated that a little less than 3,000,000 Africans have become urbanized in various degrees. In short, every year sees more Africans drawn from their tribal set-ups, and every year sees the ranks of detribalized Africans swell. Incidentally, while the Christian Church and the school are exploding colonialism, colonialism, by its aggressive economic programme, is busy exploding tribalism, and in collaboration with the Church and school, the job could not be done any better, nor any faster. If we accept the argument that African tribalism is on the way out, then the handwriting on the wall should read 'From Tribalism —what next? Of course, nationalism.'

It must be remembered, particularly in these days when people tend to look down on tribalism, that fundamentally the tribal concept arose out of a common need of a group of people who had a common goal. Since this common need is no longer there, but since a new area of common interest has been created by the colonization of Africa, a new common goal is being formulated and nationalism is the expression of that goal. The Government of the Union of South Africa is now trying to push back the African tribes into their former tribal patterns to avert this so-called danger of African nationalism, which is an amalgamation of different tribes with a common objective.

Colonial powers have helped with the detribalization of the African, and the African had to be detribalized before he could aspire nationally. He had to be purged of his narrow tribal outlook before he could be made to see beyond the tribal circle. There is now a growing tendency among Africans to think of themselves less and less as tribesmen, but more and more as Africans. The different tribes in Nigeria more and more regard themselves as Nigerians, in Ghana as Ghanaians, in Tanganyika as Tanganyikans. This point will be made clearer when we take up in the next chapter the question of African political consciousness as evidenced by African political institutions.

With the construction of good roads, bridges, and railroads, and with the introduction of motor-cars, lorries, buses, trains, and aeroplanes, the African people have become highly mobile. In many places isolation has been annihilated. With the mobility of the population, the exchange of ideas has been greatly accelerated. The dissemination of all kinds of information has been unprecedented in African history. Even the illiterate people are now better educated and better trained than ever before. The radio has revolutionized African outlook. Different parts of Africa have now been brought to the very doors of the radio-owning African. In fact, a good part of the major happenings of the world now come streaming into the African's ears. With the rise of literacy, the press made its appearance among different

African populations which have become a vital reading public. The African people read not only their thoughts but those of others separated from them by vast stretches of water. What happens in Europe, Asia, America, and Australia has become of real interest to the African people.

We may now pause and recapitulate these four points. Colonialism has created a radio audience, and the next is most likely to be a television audience. It has created a reading public. It has created a press-writing public. It has created a travelling public by land, sea, and air. All these four kinds of African public are growing by hundreds of thousands every year. Other factors receiving due consideration, the tendency has been the creation of a comparatively well-informed and enlightened African public, and a focusing of the world's problems on the public consciousness of the African people. The African public that existed before the introduction of the radio, press, train, and motor-car, was highly localized or regionalized. Particularism is now, in many places, giving way to universalism. Colonialism has given birth to a new brand of African—a non-tribal African —in short, a national African.

The formation of these four types of African public has many self-evident implications into which we shall not go to any length; but let it be noted that the tendency of radio, press-writing, reading, and travelling public is to encourage the habit of building up knowledge, comparing things and people, following ideas, and passing judgment. Men begin to judge themselves by the higher standards of others. If they find themselves wanting, they determine to improve themselves. The whole Westernization of African people is a good illustration of this point. Colonialism has engendered a vigorous spirit of progressive competition in all walks of life, and this, among others, is the legacy that colonialism has, wittingly or otherwise, bequeathed to Africa.

Let us now look at the economy of the peoples of Africa. In most areas the only medium of exchange was barter. There was no money economy to speak of. But now a new economic system has been introduced. Millions no longer have to own livestock for their subsistence. They can sell their labour, and this new moneyed class is very powerful. As one African Nyasa-lander once put it, 'Today all people do not need to have goats, cattle and sheep in order to live. They only need money. If they have money, why, they have cattle, goats and sheep right in their purses. Money is the cow that does not move, breathe, drink, and eat grass. It is a very good cow. You can milk it any time. You can eat and drink it any time. It is a cow that does many things for us.' This represents a complete mental revolution, more so when it is borne in mind that this is the attitude of a man who never saw the four corners of a classroom. Millions of Africans now have bank accounts and millions are taking out insurance policies, and this represents a growing confidence in banking institutions and insurance companies. This, again, means the emer-gence of a new type of African. A capitalistic class is growing among the African people. The African public is becoming more and more aware of the new ways of investing money.

The last of the four points we have raised is the new social and economic stratification of the African peoples. New armies of African bakers, butchers, cobblers, tailors, storekeepers, clerks, mechanics, builders, carpenters, and a chain of others have made their appearance on the scene, and they are changing the whole African social pattern. In relation to industry and commerce, the African is acquiring class consciousness as a worker. He wants his voice to be heard in industry and commerce. The birth of African trade unions is really that of the new African who believes in economic justice, and who is prepared to fight lawfully to achieve this end. It would be tedious to recount the numerous trade unions and other unions found all over Africa. The point we want to make is that European trade unionism has been transferred to the African scene. But let us here note that the African workers as a class are now painfully aware of the glaring discrepancies between European and African wages. They have become conscious of the fact that the prosperity of European-dominated Africa is largely due to them. But they have no quarrel with that. Their bone of contention is that their economic reward is far below that of the European wage-earner. A deep sense of economic exploitation afflicts the African worker. Perhaps a recourse to Alan Paton will help us to appreciate more fully the real feelings of the African worker. Alan Paton describes John Kumalo's feelings thus:

'Here in Johannesburg it is the mines, he said, everything is the mines. These high buildings, this wonderful City Hall, this beautiful Parktown with its beautiful houses, all this is built with the gold from the mines. This wonderful hospital for Europeans, the biggest hospital south of the Equator, it is built with the gold from the mines.

'There was a change in his voice, it became louder like the voice of a bull or a lion. Go to our hospital, he said, and see our people lying on the floors. They lie so close you cannot step over them. But it is they who dig the gold. For three shillings a day. We come from the Transkei, and from Basutoland, and from Bechuanaland, and from Swaziland, and from Zululand. And from Ndotsheni also. We live in the compounds. We must leave our wives and families behind. And when the new gold is found, it is not we who will get more for our labour. It is the white man's shares that will rise, and you will read it in all the papers. They go mad when gold is found. They bring more of us to live in the compounds, to dig under the ground for three shillings a day. They do not think, here is a chance to pay more for labour. They think only, here is a chance to build a bigger house and buy a bigger car. It is important, they say, for all South Africa is built on the mines.

'He growled, and his voice grew deep, it was like thunder that was rolling. But it is not built on the mines, he said, it is built on our backs, on our sweat, on our labour. Every factory, every theatre, every beautiful house, they are all built by us.'[1]

John Kumalo's remarks are true of the present situations prevalent in European-ruled Africa. The African worker is engaged in a bitter struggle to get the powers-that-be to accept the principle of equal pay for equal work.

We shall not tarry here longer than we have done. We must proceed to the next chapter and try to determine the political

[1] *Cry, the Beloved Country* (Jonathan Cape, 1948), pp. 36-7.

nature of the African himself. We have seen that colonialism has given to Africa a new vigorous industrial pattern, a new social and industrial consciousness, a new way of organizing and doing things, new skills, new insights, new dreams and visions. It has created a new climate, a new environment. It has annihilated many tribal, linguistic, ethnic barriers and divisions. It is largely responsible for the unification of African tribes, where tribal divisions had made for weakness rather than for strength. It has brought Africa into international light, and this has been very helpful if Africa is to keep pace with the rest of the world. The European colonial powers are to be greatly praised and thanked for the work they have done in helping the emergence of African nationalism. It is only a blind man who will not appreciate the fact that colonialism has fertilized, stimulated, invigorated, and shaped African nationalism. The twentieth-century African nationalism is indeed the child of European colonialism.

CHAPTER SEVEN

The African Himself

Up to this point we have not tried to paint the picture of the African in his pre-European days. We have confined our attention exclusively to external forces that are stimulating, formulating, and shaping African nationalism. In this chapter we wish to answer these questions: Did the African have any sense of freedom prior to the coming of white people to Africa? Did he treasure freedom? Was he prepared to defend it once it was actually or potentially threatened? Did the African have any democratic institutions prior to the European era in Africa? We shall defer the discussion of the last question to Chapter 8.

Many Westerners have argued again and again that freedom was introduced to Africa by the white man; that democracy was also European-introduced; that the present African clamour for freedom and for democracy is but a clamour for 'the things of the white man'. Our main task therefore is to try to determine the presence or absence of freedom and democracy ere white people came to Africa. Our leading questions are: Are freedom and democracy indigenous or alien to Africa? Is the present African struggle for independence something that was there before or after European occupation?

To answer these questions we propose to examine, broadly rather than minutely, some of the most important areas of African life—namely, philology, the institution of slavery, African history, and lastly, African legislature and judicature, both of which will be discussed in the next chapter.

African linguistics, even on a most superficial level, yield information that throws more light on our investigation. The following table will illustrate our point more clearly:

English	freedom
French	*liberté*
Portuguese	*liberdade*
Latin	*libertas*

Spanish	*libertad*
Zulu (South Africa)	*inkululeko*
Xhosa (South Africa)	*inkululeko*
Ndebele (Southern Rhodesia)	*inkululeko*
Shona (Southern Rhodesia)	*rusununguko*
Sotho (Basutoland)	*tokoloho*
Ibo (Nigeria)	*efe*
Ga (Ghana)	*henoyeli*
Ewe (Ghana)	*vovome*
Twi (Ghana)	*fawohodie*

If we examine the institution of slavery, the following table is impressive:

English	slave	slavery
French	*esclave*	*esclavage*
Portuguese	*escravo*	*escravatura*
Latin	*mancipium*	*servitus*
Spanish	*esclavo*	*esclavitud*
Zulu	*isiqgili*	*ubuqgili*
Xhosa	*isiqgini*	*ubuqgini*
Ndebele	*isiqgili*	*ubuqgili*
Shona	*nhaphwa*	*nhaphwo*
Sotho	*lekhoba*	*bokhoba*
Amharic	*baria*	*barnet*
Ibo	*oru*	*igba-oru*
Ga	*nyon*	——
Ewe	*amefele*	*kluvinyenye*
Twi	*donko*	——

Our chief interest here is not philology as such, but what light these philological data throw on our present investigation into the existence or non-existence of freedom among the African people before the advent of the white people. From these two tables it is apparent that there is no linguistic resemblance between African and European words. The African words are as un-European as the European words are un-African. There is no actual philological relationship between the European and African words. We cannot therefore escape the logical conclusion that the concept of freedom is not foreign but indigenous to Africa. To the best of our knowledge of African philology in general, and Bantu philology in particular, there is hardly an African language that has no word or phrase for freedom and slavery.

But the existence of the word freedom in the African languages we have cited so far is by no means conclusive evidence that freedom was an accomplished fact among the African people. The philological existence of freedom and slavery could be equated with that of fairy or goblin. Do these words arise out of the exuberance of imagination, or out of real-life situations? In other words, have these words an historical content or merely a fictitious one?

It is common historical knowledge that slavery existed in Africa long before white people came. The existence of two classes of people—namely, the captor and the captured, master and slave—logically implies that of freedom and unfreedom. If slavery was known to Africa before the coming of the white people, it follows that freedom was also known. Slavery is the deprivation of human freedom. Where there is no freedom there cannot be slavery. Both freedom and slavery flourished within an historical *milieu* and not within the realm of fiction. This point is useful as it throws more light on the fact that the present African struggle for independence roots back into the Africa of pre-European days, and African languages are a living testimony to this fact.

We shall now turn to African history and see what information we can extract there so that we may see whether or not such information substantiates or refutes the philological fact of the nativeness of freedom on the continent of Africa. We shall not attempt to cover all African countries. We shall take only a few samples to demonstrate that long before white people came, there were, as we have indicated elsewhere in this book, many bitter, cruel tribal wars which resulted in the subjection of some tribes by others, and in the domination of some tribes over others. We shall begin with the history of West Africa.

The history of tribal wars in West Africa is a long and complicated one, and we cannot go into it here. For a brief survey that would give a rough picture of the tribal conflicts, we refer the reader to T. R. Batten's little volume, *Tropical Africa in World History, Book Three*.[1] Here we can only highlight certain historical facts. In the Gold Coast, for instance, there were many tribes that were very hostile to one another. Very often the stronger tribe conquered the weaker tribe and deprived it of its freedom. As time went on the subject tribe would try to regain its lost independence by making an open revolt against the conqueror. Sometimes the conquered tribe sought the help of another strong tribe so that it would overthrow the domination of the victor-tribe and thus regain its lost independence. The life-and-death struggle between the Ashanti and Fanti is a good case in point. As the independence of the Fanti was constantly threatened by the Ashanti, the Fanti sought European protection to preserve their tribal integrity against the Ashanti. Incidentally, foreign protection turned out, in the long run, to be foreign domination. The same tribal struggles existed among the Yoruba and other tribes of Nigeria.

Bantu history south of the equator also reveals the same struggle between the victor and the vanquished tribe. In Zulu-land, for instance, there arose at the beginning of the last century a black military genius by the name of Shaka. Sometimes this African military genius has been called the 'Black Napoleon of South Africa'. He conquered many small tribes and made them into one Zulu nation. Then he embarked on a grand scheme of conquest. Other tribes whose sovereignty he threatened unsuccess-fully attacked him. Seeing that they could not live in complete freedom and independence while Shaka threatened them with subjection, death, and extinction, they trekked into the unknown where they hoped to live in peace and complete freedom, and thus began the Bantu migrations of the early nineteenth century. The Angoni fled from Shaka's fury and settled in what is now Nyasaland; the Shangane fled from Zululand and settled in what is now Portuguese East Africa; the Ndebele crossed the Drakens-berg Mountains and settled temporarily in what is now called

[1] Batten: *Tropical Africa in World History, Book Three* (Oxford, 1939), ch. 8.

78

the Transvaal, but harassed here by the Boers, they crossed Rudyard Kipling's 'great, grey-green, greasy Limpopo River' and settled in what is now Southern Rhodesia. The Mantati fled westwards and attacked the Bechuana, and later turned south against the Griqua, and after a thorough defeat by the latter, fled northwards and settled in the neighbourhood of the present world-renowned Victoria Falls on the Zambezi River. These were the Makololo later found here by Dr. David Livingstone.[1]

We shall not burden the reader any further with Bantu history but we want him to notice these points so that he may understand better the present trend of African nationalism. The African tribes subjected one another, that is, deprived one another of freedom, long before the white people made their influence felt on the whole continent of Africa. The tribes so subjected tried more often than not to win back their freedom. They did this by rising against the conqueror, or by joining hands against the conqueror, and if this was not feasible, the subject tribes, or the tribes threatened with subjection, fled from the conqueror to reassert their independence elsewhere. Their hearts, as they fled from the conqueror, panted and throbbed with the desire for freedom—independence. Freedom therefore was not only philologically but also historically known to Africa. The northward and westward flights of the Bantu tribes from Zululand can be compared with the general exodus of the peoples of Europe to America in the seventeenth and eighteenth centuries. The European peoples were running away from tyranny at home, and so were the Bantu tribes running away from Shaka's tyranny in Zululand. The European people wanted to found new settlements in the New World where they would be free, and so did the Bantu tribes want to found new settlements where they would be free. It would be boring to draw parallels between European and Bantu struggles for independence. Our contention is this: the African struggle for independence began long before the white man came to Africa.

The coming of European powers to Africa had certain important results. It liberated the weaker tribes from the actual

[1] T. R. Batten, op. cit., ch. 14.

or potential domination of the stronger tribes; it gave real protection to these weaker tribes, and it is common historical knowledge that many African tribes, fearful of their more powerful neighbours, often sought European protection. The European conquest of many parts of Africa therefore brought a considerable measure of independence and protection to many African tribes, but with it, it also brought the master tribes, so to speak, under immediate European domination. Both the victor and the vanquished became subjects of European powers. To begin with, this alien domination was a great relief to the once-subject tribes. It compensated for the freedom that had been lost to the ruling tribes. But this new alien domination was a thorn in the flesh to the once-master tribes. We can make this point clear by quoting what some Africans used to say during World War II when asked whether they would like to be under German rule. They said, 'It makes no difference to us to be under British or German rule. In both cases, it's foreign domination', and secretly many of these wished Germany success so that the European powers in Africa might have first-hand experience of what it feels like to live under foreign domination. In the same way the subject tribes were only too happy to see their masters also become subjects of aliens. In fact, European powers used many of these subject tribes to conquer the ruling tribes.

The new European administration, which was based on military strength, made no distinction between the once-ruler and the once-ruled. All tribes were treated in the same way. The once-ruling tribes resented being placed on equal footing with the once-subject tribes, and the subject tribes which had helped the European powers in the conquest of the ruling tribes were also equally disappointed in that the new European administration, which they had helped to set up, did not give them preferential treatment. It regarded them all as a 'bunch of natives'. This greatly helped in bringing together the hostile tribes that soon united against the new common enemy.

Another important point that we must discuss, before proceeding to trace the African efforts to regain their lost independence, is that of the parcelling out of Africa to European powers. When Africa was finally mapped out large movements of tribes became illegal. Prior to the acquisition of Africa by Europeans, if a tribe felt that it could not overthrow the ruling tribe, or that it could not defend itself against a threatening tribe, the whole tribe trekked to some other part of the territory where it would dwell in peace and freedom. But this became impossible after the occupation of Africa. Clear political boundaries now hedge them in, and above their heads looms foreign domination so that they cannot go elsewhere to reassert their independence. They are compelled to fight for it where they are now. Solution by trekking to the north or to the south is no longer possible.

Many Westerners have contended that Africans are perfectly happy under European rule, and that the present struggle against European rule is due to an educated African minority that is power-hungry. We wish to address ourselves to this part of the problem, and to do this we shall have to rely on history, for there is no other way of proving or disproving that Africans want to be ruled by the present European powers. The historical struggle to regain their lost independence, or to remove European threats to their independence, can be better appreciated by following the moves which different tribes made from time to time. Among the historical items listed in the Ghana Independence Souvenir of 6 March 1957 were the following highlights:

1817 British Mission to Ashanti.
1821 British Government took control and placed British settlements under the Sierra Leone Government.
1824 British defeated by Ashanti.
     Governor Sir Charles McCarthy killed.
1826 Ashanti defeated at Dodowa.
1873 Ashanti army defeated at Elmina.
1900 Ashanti besieged Kumasi but defeated.

The history of South Africa also affords many examples of the unwillingness of African tribes to fall under European rule. The well-known and so-called Kaffir Wars between the European settlers and the Xhosa throw more light on how African tribes from time to time endeavoured to guard their integrity against foreign invaders.

In what is now Southern Rhodesia similar uprisings occurred. In 1896 the Matabele rose against the British with the hope of regaining their independence, but failed to do so. In the same year the Mashona also made an unsuccessful revolt. They were easily quelled by British guns. As recently as 1952 the Kikuyu, who formed the bulk of the Mau Mau movement, made an attempt to regain their lost independence, but to no avail.

This is enough to show that the present European rule in Africa has, in many places, been established by European military force, and whatever acquiescence the African shows in the European rule, it is not out of design or intention, but out of necessity. In every instance where the African has tried to regain his lost independence European guns have quickly swung into action and have spoken for European domination as against African freedom. In the end the African lost faith in his spear ever bringing him his freedom which he lost to Europeans. European guns proved too strong for him. So for a while he developed a philosophy of indifference and tried to make the best of a bad job. But even his newly acquired philosophical indifference did not extinguish the spark of freedom in his heart. His heart for ever yearned for the freedom which is the birthright of every normal human being, so he tried to organize himself peacefully, since he had failed otherwise, that eventually he might regain his lost freedom. This brings us to another aspect of our discussion.

There are too many African political organizations to go into in a work of this nature, so we shall only pick out a few representative examples here and there to demonstrate that the African struggle for freedom, having failed to achieve its goal through military action, has now changed its tactics. The following list of African political movements indicates sufficiently the African's desire for freedom in the land of his birth. These movements may word their aims and objectives in different ways, and they may employ different methods in achieving these aims and objectives, yet they all have one thing in common—to regain their lost freedom:

1. The African National Congress of South Africa.
2. The United Gold Coast Convention which was superseded by Dr. Kwame Nkrumah's C.P.P. in 1950.
3. The Tanganyika African National Union.
4. The Uganda African National Congress.
5. The Northern Rhodesia African National Congress.
6. The Nyasaland African National Congress.
7. The Southern Rhodesia African National Congress.
8. The Kenya African Congress.

We shall repeat here that these all-African political organizations emerged as the result of the Africans' failures to regain their freedom by military action, and as a result of the African's love for freedom. These African organizations are trapped and crippled from time to time by adverse European legislation which is deliberately directed towards rendering them ineffective as organs for securing African political freedom. But despite all this, these organizations have not lost sight of their main objective— African freedom. This point will become more clear when we summarize some of the programmes that have been planned and executed by some of these organizations.

The African National Congress of South Africa, then the Bantu Congress of South Africa, began in 1912. This Congress came about as the result of the Act of Union of Cape Colony, Natal, Orange Free State and the Transvaal, in 1910, which 'made it plain that the African was not to be accepted as a citizen in the Union. Race and colour were to be absolute and permanent criteria by which to assess human worth.'[1] This further threat to the freedom of the African soon united the once hostile tribes, and hence Zulu, Xhosa, Sotho, Shangane, and Venda sank their tribal identities and joined hands as African people who stood against the African-downgrading European rule.

In 1913 the Government of the Union of South Africa passed the Land Act introducing rural residential segregation. To combat this obnoxious Act, the Congress raised money, and in 1914 dispatched a strong and representative deputation to England to

[1] *Africa South*, Oct.–Dec. 1956, p. 71.

plead for the African cause. But the deputation failed. The Congress has been active despite strong official opposition. In 1952 it organized passive resistance against all discriminatory legislation in South Africa, and this landed in jail thousands of Africans who were prepared to buy freedom through suffering; but the Government was too strong for the Congress. It damped down African resistance to its own will.

The Gold Coast (now Ghana) also affords a good study of African political movements aiming at securing freedom for the African people. The United Gold Coast Convention also came into existence for the purpose of securing African political freedom. In 1949, however, this political organization was succeeded by the newly formed Convention People's Party, and it is this Party that swept Dr. Kwame Nkrumah into power in 1951, and it is this Party that was responsible for the creation of the new independent state of Ghana (6 March 1957). Its motto right from the beginning was 'Self-government now'.

At the beginning of this chapter we asked ourselves this question: Did the African people, prior to the coming of the white people to Africa, have any conception of freedom? Philologically, we have demonstrated the existence of freedom before the coming of white people to Africa. We have also shown historically how the African struggled to regain and maintain his independence before and after European occupation of Africa. The African struggle for independence is as old as the European struggle for their independence. In short, the concept of political freedom is as native to Africa as the native African himself. The European powers succeeded temporarily in suppressing the African's desire for independence, but, to borrow the language of another, in the unconscious the suppressed wish still exists, only waiting for its chance to become active.[1] African nationalism, as we have stated elsewhere, is this European-suppressed African desire to rule themselves, reasserting itself against hostile circumstances. In the struggle for their independence, Africans are not fighting for 'the things of the white man', but for their things which the white man, to put it bluntly, stole away from them.

[1] Sigmund Freud: *An Outline of Psychoanalysis* (Hogarth, 1949), p. 40.

If there is anything at all that the present African nationalism proves, it is that the African is as freedom-loving as the Europeans and Americans themselves. It serves no good purpose for Westerners to think that freedom is only good for the white man and not for the African people. African philology and history show clearly that the African believes in freedom, that he fights for freedom, that he suffers for it, and that he dies for it. African nationalism is really an address to European powers—'GIVE US BACK OUR FREEDOM'. And the whole struggle in Africa revolves around this demand. European powers, in most cases, are refusing to give back the African people their independence.

Mr. Basil Davidson, British author and journalist, is right when he says:

'Today, many people talk of the need for Europeans to make concessions and gestures which will help win confidence in European leadership. But the African does not ask for concessions, nor need gestures of European generosity. He is not asking for privileges. The African is asking for his rights. He seeks to establish equality of all individuals, black, brown or white. In this demand there can be no half-way compromise, for it is either absolute equality or superiority of one over the other.'[1]

[1] *Report on Southern Africa* (Jonathan Cape, 1952), pp. 71-2.

CHAPTER EIGHT

African Governments

One of the burning questions today is: Did the African have any democracy before the coming of the white man to Africa? Many Europeans and Americans contend that Africans never had democracy until the coming of the white man. In other words, it is the white man who introduced democracy to Africa. And so we find many Europeans and Americans arguing, 'Suppose Africans were given their independence, would they carry on their governments on a democratic basis? Can the Africans understand democracy which is essentially the white man's way of government?' Like every good thing in this world, democracy is mistakenly thought of as having white origin. Historical facts, however, show that democracy is not a monopoly of the white people. Other races have also had their democratic institutions long before coming into contact with the Western world. For our purpose, however, we shall confine ourselves to the continent of Africa where the nativeness of democracy is much in dispute.

Those of us who have lived in Africa know that the African people are democratic to a point of inaction. Things are never settled until everyone has had something to say. African councils allow the free expression of all shades of opinions. Any man has full right to express his mind on public questions. Even those in authority will always consult public opinion. '*Batini abantu?*' (Ndebele, Southern Rhodesia) means 'What do the people say?' '*Nxa abantu bevuma, kulungile*' means 'If people agree, that is all right'. The people—the common people—are the basis of all properly constituted authority, although many European and American observers think that the chief is the basis of African authority. The real trouble with African institutions was that they were democratic to a fault, and this, in a way, has held the people down, since to carry out any programme required the sanction of the whole clan or tribe.

86

We are aware, however, that many Bantu languages do not have a corresponding word for democracy, but the absence of this word must not be taken to mean the absence of the essence of democracy among the peoples of Africa, just as the absence of a pure Anglo-Saxon word for democracy does not necessarily mean the absence of democracy among the Anglo-Saxon peoples. The Spanish *democracia*, the French *démocratie*, the Dutch *democratie*, the German *demokrati*, the Portuguese *democracia*, and the Afrikaans *demokrasie*, all prove that there is no pure word for democracy in these languages. Etymologically, the word democracy comes from Greek *demokratia* (*demos* the people, *kraiten* to rule), but this does not mean that other nationalities had no idea of democracy. It merely means these nations borrowed the Greek word to express an idea that was already among them. The Ndebele of Southern Rhodesia like *ukuzibusa* (to rule themselves). Similarly, the Shona of the same country like *kuzwitonga* (self-determination). We now want to trace African democracy in the actual institutions of the people, and to do this we shall make a brief survey of their judicial systems and then turn to their political institutions.

One of the difficulties confronting the Westerners, in their attempt to understand African customs and laws, is that there is no African literature extending over many centuries as in the case of the European literature which is traceable into the B.C. period. Because of this absence of African literature, many Westerners come to the wrong conclusion that the African tribes never had any legal system. They argue that there are no written records to be found in African courts, and this is true; but that does not mean that Africans had no clearly defined judicial systems. While the European depends on recording in black and white what happens, the illiterate African records what happens in his native memory. The laws of the people live in their consciousness, but this does not mean that theirs is a better way of recording. The European way of recording is definitely superior to that of the African tribes. But what we want to point out is that most African legal systems we have studied show that in many places African judicature was highly developed. Many anthropological studies undertaken by European and American scholars support this fact. Our own personal observation of the operation of Native law also proves to us how highly developed many African legal systems were long before the white man came to Africa. An interesting article by S. F. Nadel appeared under the title, 'Reason and Unreason in African Law'.[1] Among other things, the article stated:

'The Lozi,[2] though still without a written code, possess councils on legislation and councils meeting as courts, elaborate court procedures, and indeed a whole legal philosophy. . . .

'For Lozi law, far from being vitiated by crudities of evidence, by superstitions and biases of various kinds, is governed by clear methods of reasoning and rigorous judicial logic.'

In most African legal systems we have consulted and have actually seen in operation, there are many clearly stated laws relating to inter-personal relations, marriage and family, strangers, inter-tribal relations, property, and society in general. Universities in Africa offer Native law as a special course of study. British magistrates with whom we have had occasion to discuss points of difference and similarity between English law and Ndebele law, for instance, have admitted that while in some respects the English law is superior to the Ndebele law, yet their experience in Southern Rhodesian native courts had convinced them beyond doubt that in other respects the English law is inferior to the Ndebele law.

Among the Shona of Southern Rhodesia, cases may be tried by the head of the family. An appeal can be made to the headman, and from here an appeal can be made to the chief. Family heads, village heads and chiefs try only specified cases. For example, a serious crime like murder could not be tried by the head of the family or the head of a group of villages, only by the chief. Cases were tried by any one of these three courts according to the degree of their seriousness. This is a general principle found among most African judicial systems. *Dare* is the Shona word for council. The Rhodesian Ndebele is *ibandla*. The Zulu of Natal,

[1] *Africa*, vol. XXVI, no. 2, April 1956.
[2] A native tribe of Northern Rhodesia.

88

the Xhosa of the Cape Province, and the Tswana of Bechuanaland use *ibandla*, *ibunga*, and *kgotla* respectively, for the same word. This African council preceded European advent in Africa. In origin, composition, and procedure it is entirely African.

At the *dare*, which was usually held in the open air, the chief or his representative, together with the leading men of his area, tried *moswa* (case). Any adult man was welcome to the *dare* to listen to the proceedings. The defendant and the complainant and their relatives and friends came along to the *dare*. Disinterested persons other than women and children also came to the *dare* to hear and learn as men tried the case. The complainant first laid bare 'that which troubled him against the accused'. After that the accused spoke in his own behalf. Both parties spoke without interruption. After the two parties had spoken, witnesses gave 'that which they knew' about the case. This would then be followed by a long cross-examination by any one of the leading men of the *dare*, but great care was always taken not to *manikidza* (force) the accused. Where it was obvious that the accused did not mean what he said, the men straightened that out for him, and with his approval. The whole hearing took sometimes half a day, or a full day, or many days, depending upon the nature of the case. At the end of the whole hearing, the chief or his representative would summarize the case in the light of the evidence given by both parties. At the conclusion of his summary he delivered the verdict in the presence of the people, *Wadyiwa nemoswa* (the case has eaten you, i.e. you are found guilty).

There were no lawyers employed. The law was simple. The procedure was equally simple but very effective. The native courts of justice were open to the rich and the poor alike. The presence of the relatives and friends of both parties ensured real justice, but we are quite aware that miscarriage of justice was not unknown in native courts. This procedure was and is still quite common among many African tribes.

The opening of a Ndebele *ibandla* is quite interesting. One of the leading men, chosen by the rest of the men, will silence the open-air gathering in this manner, and I quote this from Ndebele procedure:

'Tulani, mahlabezulu. Sesiqalisa umsebenzi katesi. Hlalani pansi lonke liti cwaka, isingena indaba manje. Akutetwa muntu, hatshi; kutetwa icala kupela. Umuntu lecala akuhambelani.'

(Be quiet, ye people. We now begin the work. Sit down all of you and be dead silent, the hearing is about to begin. It is not the person that is to be tried, no; it is the case that is to be tried. A person and a case do not go together.)

The Ndebele court maintains a very serious tone from start to finish. Any disrespect shown may result in a fine on the ground that the culprit 'does not respect the *ibandla* [council]'. Although Ndebele like humour, they see to it that it is kept out of the court, and anyone who drags it into the court can only do so at his own risk. Hence the Ndebele will try, for hours, a case that has many humorous aspects without even betraying a slight smile, and laugh heartily when they get to their villages after the hearing. To a Ndebele an *indaba*—a case—is a very serious matter, because you *dunga impilo yomuntu*—you disturb the life of a human being. Humour, therefore, is interpreted in such circumstances as light-mindedness, and light-mindedness in dealing with the life of another human being is to treat the individual *njengenja* (like a dog). (Among the Ndebele a dog certainly does not get justice.)

Among the Yoruba people of Nigeria, the opening of the court runs along somewhat similar lines to those among the Rhodesian Ndebele:

'Ka gbohun, Atoto o, Arere o, Ki Oniko pa iko re mo, K'abiyamo toju omo re, Ki elenu pa enu re mo, Okun aiye ja, Okun ore meji ja, Okun ebi ja, awon agbagba fe tun so, enikeni to ba di nwon lowo, awon agba yio je e niya.'

(Be civil, be quiet, be dumb, let the cougher conceal (or refrain from) coughing; let women with babes take care of their babes (keep them from crying). Let everybody close his mouth. The cord that binds humanity is broken; the big men now want to tie up the broken cords; and if anyone disturbs them in this work of reorganization, such disturber shall be seriously dealt with.)[1]

[1] A. K. Ajisafe: *The Laws and Customs of the Yoruba People* (Routledge), p. 43.

The author of the above quotation points out that anyone who disturbs the court is held up for contempt of court. He may be fined or punished by other means—namely, flogging or imprisonment. Most of the African courts are marked by serious-ness in their proceedings, and by the fact that it is not only one man who tries the case, but a group of men. All native courts derive their authority, not from the chief, not even from the big men, but from the people—the common people. The verdict of the jury had to satisfy the common sense, the customary laws of the people, or else real violence would break out once the common people became convinced that the big men were only twisting the customs of the people to suit their own whims, and it was the big men themselves who would normally suffer in the event of an outbreak of physical violence. The man who stands by what is just is a hero in the eyes of many Africans. The Rhodesian Shona regard a justice-loving man as *mwari*, God. The Rhodesian Ndebele call him *inkosi*, king. Albert Schweitzer shows a good grasp of the moral position of the African when he says:

'The Negro is not in a position to estimate what these technical conquests of nature mean as proofs of mental and spiritual superiority, but on one point he has an unerring intuition, and that is on the question whether any particular white man is a real, moral personality or not. If the native feels that he is this, moral authority is possible; if not, it is simply impossible to create it. The child of nature, having been not artificialized and spoiled as we have been, has only elementary standards of judgment, and he measures us by the most elementary of them all, the moral standard. Where he finds goodness, justice and genuineness of character, real worth and dignity, that is, behind the external dignity given by social circumstances, he bows and acknowledges his master; where he does not find them he remains really defiant in spite of all appearance of submission.'[1]

This same observation is made by various European authori-ties who have had first-hand relationships with the African. In a brochure entitled *Your Servant and You*, issued to European

[1] Charles R. Joy: *Albert Schweitzer: An Anthology* (Black, 1952), p. 186.

immigrants to the Federation of Rhodesia and Nyasaland, the Public Relations Department makes, among other things, this warning, 'The most important thing of all that you should do is to adopt the right attitude towards the African. He [the African] naturally looks for courtesy and justice.'

It is obvious from what we have said that the African peoples had their own system of justice long before the white people came. The concept of justice and the system and practice of justice were not European-introduced to Africa. These were born the day the African was born in Africa. It serves no good purpose for Westerners to maintain the fiction that 'the African has no sense of justice. If he's given freedom, injustice will reign all over Africa.'

The next question we want to answer is: Did democracy exist among the African people before the coming of the white people? This question is very pertinent since many Westerners often wonder, 'Can the African be trusted to be democratic if he's given freedom and independence? Does he know democracy in the sense of the West?'

It would be idle and unprofitable for us to attempt to answer the last question since democratic procedures vary even in the same Western democracies. In Britain, members of Parliament are elected for not more than five years; in the U.S.A. congressmen are elected for a fixed period of two years and senators for six, while the President is elected for four years. British observers have repeatedly admitted that they do not understand American politics. This is also true of American observers with regard to British politics. The world at large is puzzled by French politics that are, to all appearances, so unstable. British democracy is often associated with socialism, and American democracy with capitalism. At the head of British democracy is a constitutional monarch, while at the head of American democracy is a president. But despite this external divergence, democracy in all these countries has one common factor: in a democracy the source of the authority of the government rests with the common people. The people have a right to make and unmake kings or presidents, to vote legislators into and out of power.

In brief, democracy is the will of the people. Those who govern, govern with the free consent of the governed. Democracy to be democracy therefore does not need the same externals, or mechanics, but it needs one 'soul', and that is the will of the majority. In fact, democracy is the majority-voice in the running of any country be it in Europe, Asia, America, or Africa.

African politics centre round the king or the chief, depending upon the tribe in question. Who elected the African chief to the position of authority? The method of election or appointment will reveal to the reader whether or not African chieftainship or kingship was dictatorial or democratic. In the Gold Coast (now Ghana) the law of enstoolment whereby the chief was enthroned, and the law of destoolment whereby the chief was dethroned, are too well known to need elaboration. The power to elect the chief was vested in the people—the common people—and since it was they who were responsible for his creation, the common people were also vested with the power to dismiss the chief in the event of his abusing his people-given authority. At the time of enstoolment, the enstooler was ordered by the people to convey their wishes to the new chief as follows:

> Tell him that
>> We do not wish greediness.
>> We do not wish that he should curse us.
>> We do not wish that his ears should be hard of hearing.
>> We do not wish that he should call people fools.
>> We do not wish that he should act on his own initiative.
>> We do not wish things done as in Kumasi.
>> We do not wish that it should ever be said, 'I have no time. I have no time.'
>> We do not wish personal abuse.[1]

Clearly, the people were trying to guard against tyranny that could only result in their abuse by the chief. The people wanted the chief to listen to the voice of the people, and to act on their, not his, initiative. The chief was expected to respect the wishes of his people. However, human nature being what it is, the chief

[1] David E. Apter: *The Gold Coast in Transition* (Princeton University Press), p. 108, as quoted therein.

sometimes disregarded the wishes of the people. But people were not left powerless. Those who had elected him had the power to destool him and enstool another to whom they gave the same message about respecting the wish of the people. Rattray comments thus:

'If, after his election, a chief behaves in an unbecoming manner, his elders warn him privately that his behaviour is alienating his subjects and bringing the stool in disrepute. The type of conduct complained of in this manner is usually excessive drinking, going after other men's wives, being overbearing in dealing with his subjects, neglecting the advice of his elders, or getting in a rage and flogging the young men. Individual complaints against the chief are heard privately by the elders and they may ask the chief to pacify the offended person.'[1]

It is obvious that the chief was dependent upon his elders for his office, and the elders were also dependent upon the common people for the office they held. In other words, it was in the interest of the chief to be as popular with his subjects as he could. Here we see the essence of popular government. In the final analysis, the chief owed his authority to the common people. Little wonder that Rattray comes to the conclusion that among the Ashanti the constitution was, in correct practice, 'democratic to a degree'.

The Yoruba of Nigeria also afford a good example of African kingship. The king was the paramount ruler, chiefs and other notables being subordinate to him, but he ruled and governed through them. The king's advisers were responsible for the different parts of the country. The king, naturally, came from the royal house. He had enormous powers which were vested in him by the customs and laws of his country. But he was in no way despotic. The people saw to it that they did not remain at the mercy of the king. For instance, the king had power to declare war, but if his military expedition miscarried, the king was expected, under the laws of the country, to die before his defeated army returned home.[2] If he did not kill himself, the

[1] *Ashanti Law and Constitution* (Oxford, 1929), p. 82.
[2] Ajisafe, op. cit., p. 21.

people saw to it that the laws of the country were carried out, and this could only be done by the people killing the king. Thus the right to declare war on any tribe carried with it a very grave responsibility. Declaration of war meant either victory or death for the king.

On the other hand, however, if a king or a chief or a notable man became unpopular with the people, i.e. when people grew tired of the tyrannical and evil ways of the king or chief or some important person, the people had recourse to the *kirikiri* custom whereby a mob paraded through the country, or town, 'singing vituperative songs and loudly abusing' the king or chief or man they did not like. When the mob got to the quarters of their object, they threw sand and stones into his palace or house to tell him that he was no longer wanted by the people. Such a parade usually took place at night and continued for three months. Within this period the person in question was expected to reconcile himself with the people, or leave the country, or commit suicide. If he ignored or slighted the *kirikiri* display, a select body of masked, powerful men were authorized to seize the person by night and kill him.[8]

No doubt, this may sound crude to our twentieth-century ears, but one thing remains clear above everything else: among the Yoruba, as among other African tribes, the king or chief was not above the law but under the law. The common people with whom he had to be popular were the source of all his authority.

We shall now give the last example of African kingship. King Lobengula of the Southern Rhodesian Ndebele has often been called the Black Autocrat, and this is not unfair. The Ndebele were a military people living under a strict military discipline, and yet even under this system the king owed his authority to the people. He was not above the law but under the law, although in many cases he unsuccessfully tried to get the people to follow his way. On one occasion, for instance, Lobengula issued an order that a certain woman be killed. He sent two men to execute the royal order. When the two executioners reached the military district after four days hard walking, they

[8] Ajisafe, op. cit.

95

found the woman with her baby strapped on to her back. They asked her to unstrap the baby, but the woman said that if they meant to kill her, they should kill her together with her baby, and the two executioners did so, and returned to the royal kraal where now stands the modern Bulawayo.

But when the men of this military district heard of the incident they dressed up in their battle array, and, with spear and shield in hand, marched to the royal kraal and demanded the reason why the King had killed the baby. The King became so infuriated about this action that he ordered the pick of his men to get ready for battle. But he was surprised when they too demanded the explanation for the killing of the baby. 'I did not order that the baby be killed. I only ordered the death of the woman', King Lobengula said. Both sides with spears brandishing in the air roared with approval and demanded the death of the two men. The King loved his two executioners, and he hesitated to deliver them, but the armies roared their demand, and finally the King delivered the two men to suffer the fate of the baby. Justice had been done, and the men returned home, thus proving that the King could not be above the wishes of the people.

King Lobengula had a statesmanlike adviser, Lotshe kaHlaba-ngana, who had carefully sized up the military strength of the British forces and who advised him not to attack the British settlers in his country. The King, having a very shrewd intuition, agreed with Lotshe. At the council of war the debate whether or not to attack the white invaders ensued. Both the King and Lotshe strongly opposed the idea of attacking the white invaders. The people became thoroughly convinced that Lotshe was a traitor to his country and he was duly condemned to death, and the people forced the King to declare war. Thus, in 1893, the famous Matabele War broke out against the British forces, much against the King's judgement and wish—demonstrating once more that the Ndebele King had no voice of his own. His only true voice was that of his people. The Ndebele say, 'INkosi ngabantu. Ukuhlonipa iNkosi yikuzihlonipa. Odelela iNkosi yetu uyasidelela. Odumisa iNkosi yetu udumisa tina. INkosi yiti.' (The King is the people. To respect the King is to respect oneself. He who despises our King despises us. He who praises our King praises us. The King is us.)

When any Ndebele king dies, the Ndebele people say, '*Intaba idilikile*'. (The mountain has fallen.) The king was considered as the prodigious mountain of the people's customs, laws, history, security, and aspirations. In other words, the king was king because he embodied clearly what was in his people, so that if the king failed to reflect this, the people defied him. African history has many cases of this nature. A king to be king at all had to be acceptable to his people. When King Shaka of the Zulu became unacceptable to many of his people, the people left him and went to serve other kings more acceptable to them. Finally, when Shaka became more unacceptable he was assassinated to appease the conscience of the people. At the basis of all African political institutions there was the principle of popular government running through and through. It is bad history and bad civics to say the African never had democracy until the coming of the white man to Africa.[1]

From our discussion it is now obvious that the African king owed his authority to the people and that the African chief and his advisers also owed their authority to the people. The idea of a constitutional monarchy or a constitutional chief is 100 per cent, though not exclusively, African. The idea of popular government is also as African as it is European or American. Even in such a small unit as a village popular government could be clearly observed. The subject had complete freedom to move to another village if he was not satisfied with the headman of his village, and thus a headman who had more persons in his village was regarded with envy by other headmen who had fewer people. Village politics centred around the conception of popular government. Similarly, a chief who had more villages under his jurisdiction enjoyed social and political prestige, and to gain this popularity the chief had to be acceptable to his people, because if he was not acceptable, then many people, exercising their

---

[1] Among the Swazi and the Bechuana the chief was below the law and could be tried by his own council if he broke the law. See Kuper: *An African Aristocracy* (Oxford), p. 63, and Schapera: *Handbook of Tswana Law and Custom* (Oxford, 1955), p. 84.

customary right of being where they like to be, and of not being where they do not like to be, would go elsewhere. Hardly any African institution we have examined failed to prove to us that all these institutions owed their real authority to the people and not to the office-holders. If the essence of democracy is *intando yabantu* (the will of the people) then African people have had it since the dawn of their history.

But we intend pursuing the question a little further. Did the European powers introduce democracy to Africa? Superficial observation may associate the presence of white people in Africa with democracy. Outsiders may think that white people in Africa are teaching Africans, by precept and example, democratic methods. This is far from being true. What they are teaching the African is dictatorship, since they rule not according to the voice of the majority, but according to that of a minority. Therefore, whatever democracy exists in the consciousness of the African, it is not the result of coming into contact with Western democrats. The African did not come into contact with the European people on a democratic, but on a dictatorial level. The European dictated and still dictates to the African. It is therefore not correct to say it was the white man who introduced democracy to Africa, who taught the African to be democratic. We are, however, not ignoring the fact that the many material improvements and general enlightenment the Westerners brought to Africa have improved African democracy. We have no quarrel with this part of it. What we wish to refute here in unequivocal terms is the erroneous statement that democracy was European-introduced to Africa. This is not true. Democracy is as native as the African native himself.

After all, what is democracy? Is it as complex as it is often made to appear? Not at all. In a family, people agree to stick together. In a clan they agree to stick together. In a tribe they agree to stick together. In a nation they agree to stick together. Where people agree to stick together there will democracy be found. To say democracy never existed in Africa is another way of saying that people in Africa never agreed to stick together on their own initiative. The existence of African families, tribes, and nations refutes this. When people agree to stick together, that is democracy. When they are forced to stick together, that is dictatorship. It does not require military strength, or technological advancement, to have democracy; it only requires the will of the majority of the people. There is nothing supernatural or magical about democracy. It is as common to the common man as the desire to feel secure is common to all of us.

We have seen that the African ruler owed his power to the people themselves. They elected him, and by the same token they dismissed him from his office if they were dissatisfied with him. On the other hand, however, European powers in Africa are a law to themselves. They were self-appointed to their present positions of authority. European governments are responsible only to the European minority and not to the African majority. The African cannot dismiss them from any position of authority. The European is outside the law when it comes to dealing with Africans.

But it may be objected that European rule in Africa has made the fullest use of native authorities, and therefore the Africans can carry on their democratic way of life which they used to have before the white man came to Africa. There is one big difference, however. Prior to the coming of the white people, African kings, chiefs and other native authorities were ultimately responsible to the people, not to a foreign power as now is the case. The present African chiefs no longer represent the will of the people, but that of a foreign power. In other words, European powers, while preserving the shell of African kingship and chieftainship, have emptied African kingship and chieftainship of their real content. Their real authority is no longer delegated to them by their own people but by European powers. Viewed from this angle, therefore, African nationalism is a stand against European dictatorship, and a fight for democracy which the peoples of Africa once enjoyed. They want *kuzwitonga* (self-determination) *ukuzibusa* (to rule themselves) as they used to.

CHAPTER NINE

European Misconceptions

Many books on Africa have been written by European and American authors in which, consciously or unconsciously, the true picture of the African situation is distorted. Half-baked, demonstrably untrue, and mischievously misleading conclusions are drawn by some of these writers, and it is necessary to refute some of the sweeping statements made so that the reading public may get a truer picture. We shall select for this purpose a book by Stuart Cloete called *The African Giant* because, to our mind, it typifies the attitude of many Europeans.

In *The African Giant* Cloete sets out to discover whether or not the African is ready for self-government, and he comes to the conclusion that he is not ready. But to do this he paints a picture to his own taste, and *that*, he says, is the African. With regard to Rhodesia, for instance, he says, 'Where can Africans go here? How far? The sky is the limit in Rhodesia if they have brains and integrity.'[1]

Cloete forgets that with the African in Rhodesia, and elsewhere, where the doctrine of white supremacy is the rule, things are so arranged that the European must remain high and the African low. Salaries and wages are so determined that Europeans, for the same occupation and same qualifications and efficiency, get higher, and Africans lower, pay. Key positions are European prerogatives. In hotels, public parks, on the railway and on the bus, Africans—civilized or uncivilized, educated or uneducated —are discriminated against in a most humiliating manner. While there is a qualified franchise in Southern Rhodesia, the economic structure of the country is so arranged that the African finds it very difficult to qualify economically. It is more true to say that in Rhodesia the true limit of the African is the ceiling that is set by the demands of white supremacy.

Cloete goes on:

[1] *The African Giant* (Collins, 1956), p. 35.

'I was told that the Matabele had forty names for cattle, every minor variation having been distinguished by name. There is no word here for "Thank you", for the people are without the concept that requires its use. With the African, service to a relative or clansman is expected. Food cannot be refused so there is no need to thank the giver since he too, if he passes another kraal, is entitled to the same hospitality, whereas for the stranger nothing is ever done without payment.'[1]

This is a Cloete brand of Matabele, not the Rhodesian Ndebele (Matabele) among whom I was born and trained, and among whom I lived for thirty-four years. The Ndebele parents take particular pains in training their children to say 'Thank you' whenever they are given something. When a Ndebele gives a child something, she will say, 'What do you say?' and she will not let go the gift until the child has said 'Thank you'. That is how I was brought up; that is how my Ndebele wife was brought up; that is how we have brought up our children; and that is how every Ndebele child is brought up. A Ndebele mother will nearly always say to her child, 'When so-and-so gave you such-and-such, what did you say?' If the child says, 'I said, "Thank you"', the mother is satisfied. If, on the other hand, the child says, 'I didn't say anything', the mother sends the child back to thank the giver.

Cloete's statement that there is no word for 'Thank you' is too wrong to require elaborate comment, but for the benefit of our reader we give the following list which can be verified with any African linguist:

English	thank you
Ndebele (S. Rhodesia)	*ngiyabonga*
Shona (S. Rhodesia)	*ndinotenda*
Luganda (Uganda)	*webale*
Hausa (Nigeria)	*godiya*
Tswana (Bechuanaland)	*kea itumela*
Sotho (Basutoland)	*en, ahe!*

Cloete should have left the question of Ndebele anthropology to those European and American authorities who have studied

[1] Op. cit., p. 37.

the question objectively. He knows that in general all mankind say, 'Thank you', but he is anxious to make the African look basically different from other people so that he can say, 'The African is not ready for self-government'. This point will become clearer as we examine more Cloeteisms.

Cloete is not correct when he says food may not be refused. Food may or may not be refused, but in either case this is followed by 'Thank you'. The statement, '. . . for the stranger nothing is ever done without payment', is another misleading Cloeteism that does great injustice to the culture of the African people. The Ndebele hospitality is epitomized in their proverbs, which any student of the Ndebele language and customs will readily understand:

1. *Isisu somhambi asinganani.* (The stomach of a stranger is very small.)
2. *Inkomo edlulayo kayiqed' utshani.* (The passing cow does not finish the pasture.)
3. *Siyizihambi sonke.* (We are all strangers, i.e. We may as well treat one another well.)
4. *Ukupat' isihambi kuhle yikuzibekela.* (To treat a stranger well is to make provision for oneself, since one day one may also be a stranger.)

The Shona tribe of Southern Rhodesia says proverbially, '*Zhara shura mweni*', meaning, 'Only the arrival of a stranger can satisfy my enormous hunger'. This refers to the extravagant eating which is the usual way the Shona entertain a stranger.

Among the Ndebele and the Shona a stranger is accorded special status. The Ndebele call him *Umuntu kaMlimu*—the man of God; the Shona call him *Munhu waMwari*' meaning the same thing. This is as much as to say, 'Woe unto him who will not treat well the man of God'. Most African tribes we have studied treat a stranger more or less in the same way. For instance, the Yoruba of Nigeria afford another good case in point. A. K. Ajisafe says:

'The native custom in its purity is that no visitor or stranger on friendly terms must go unentertained with kola nuts and drinkables or food and lodging free. The kola nuts and the drinkables are taken together by the host and the guest. . . . A man who will not entertain his visitor or stranger . . . is believed to be mischievous, is shunned and treated with disrespect by the community.'[1]

I have been a stranger in many parts of Africa, and I have enjoyed hospitality, but this is not to say hospitality is exclusively an African trait. Far from it. I have travelled in Italy and in the U.S.A. and I have found the same hospitality extended to me. Hospitality is not a monopoly of one particular race as Cloete would have us believe. It is universal. The African has been richly blessed with this human trait.

Cloete says without qualification:

'But let us have no illusions. The black man hates the white. Above all he hates him for being white, because this is something he can never be.'[2]

Nothing could be further from the truth. Interracial societies and clubs are on the increase all over Africa. On a purely human basis the African accepts the white man. In the majority of cases, it is the white man who does not accept the African. One of the reasons why the white man fears granting the African full independence is that the African may use against the white man the hateful methods he has seen the white man use against the African. What the African hates in the white man is his unfair social, economic, political, and educational discriminatory practices which relegate the African to second- or third-rate citizenship in the land of his birth. The African hates the white man's arrogance, his mania for humiliating him in the land of his birth. The white man possesses most of the land, and he gives the African the poorest. Politically, the white man dominates the African; economically, he exploits him; socially, he degrades his human status. The African hates the fact that 150,000,000 Africans are placed at the mercy of less than 5,000,000 Europeans. It is these things that the African hates, and not the white man himself.

[1] *Laws and Customs of the Yoruba People*, pp. 94–5.
[2] Op. cit., p. 373.

There is no better way to deal with Cloete's erroneous conclusions than to quote him directly and deal with each statement as it comes. Cloete says, 'They [the educated Africans] are neither trusted nor liked by their own people'.[1] Before we give evidence to refute this we want to make some remarks on some of the aspects of African mentality which a superficial observer cannot detect. There is a great deal of truth in what Cloete says about (some) educated Africans being unacceptable to their own people; but others are acceptable. What is the reason for this? African people, in the main, accept those educated Africans who stand for African interests, and not those who further European interests at the expense of African interests. This is also true in the case of white people. Any white people who seek the true interests of the Africans are acceptable to them, but the white people who seek to exploit Africans are quite unacceptable to most Africans. An educated African who poses as leader of the people, but in whose background there is a white man who tells him what to do, is never trusted by the people. He is just a smart alec. They want a leader whose authority comes from themselves and not from a group of white people. A white man who gets his authority from the people themselves enjoys their trust and confidence. It is the case of the old proverb—'Honesty is the passport into every man's heart'. If the educated African is dishonest, he is distrusted and disliked and the same thing is true in the case of a dishonest white man. Africans trust and like educated African leaders, but not European puppets or stooges.

Prime Minister Kwame Nkrumah of Ghana affords a good example of an educated African who is trusted and liked by his own people. Prior to his accession to power as Prime Minister of the then Gold Coast, the British Administration jailed him and other educated Africans of his political party for what were considered subversive political activities. The British Administration tried to paint him as a criminal, trouble-maker, and a man to be shunned. The elections were conducted while he, as leader of his party, was in jail. His party emerged victorious. The prisoner became Prime Minister overnight. This was because the

[1] Op. cit., p. 288.

African people trust and like those educated Africans who truly stand for African interests. The creation of the state of Ghana, whose government consists of only educated Africans chosen by the people, dismisses as idle Cloete's assertion that educated Africans are neither trusted nor liked by their own people. In Nigeria most of the political powers are now in the hands of educated African leaders who have been chosen by their own people. In Kenya, Tom Mboya is an undisputed trade union leader of African workers. Mr. Wellington Chirwa, M.P., of Nyasaland, is one of the outstanding African leaders enjoying the trust and love of his fellow-Nyasalanders. Nay, it is only a man who is blind to current African affairs who fails to see that educated Africans, on the whole, enjoy throughout Africa the confidence and love of their own people, and the emergence of African nationalism which is led by the educated Africans, and which derives its real support from the masses, is sufficient evidence to prove that African people love and trust their own educated people. More and more African parents and guardians are sending their children to school, and African demand for education is greater than the supply. This is to say African people appreciate their own educated people.

Cloete is at pains to paint the African as horrible as he possibly can:

'The African has been conditioned by centuries of savage competitive life to seize what he desires wherever he can find it.'[1]

We do not deny this. This is absolutely true. We have nothing to add to or subtract from it. What concerns us here is the context in which he makes this statement. He wants to give the false impression that it is *only* the African who has been so conditioned. We could reverse his statement so that it is equally applicable to any race in this world, namely, the European has been conditioned by centuries of savage competitive life to seize what he desires wherever he can find it. The occupation of Asia, Africa, the Americas, Australasia, and other non-European lands by Europeans is an historically irrefutable piece of evidence that the European 'has been conditioned by centuries of savage com-

[1] Op. cit., p. 235.

petitive life to seize what he desires wherever he can find it'. The European settlers of Australia killed off many Aborigines. The European settlers of the Americas killed off many Indians to make room for themselves. The early Dutch settlers at the Cape hunted Bushmen as they hunted wild beasts.

In Europe, the devastating Franco-Prussian War broke out in 1870. Needless for us to quote the Napoleonic era (1799-1815) during which hundreds of thousands of lives were lost as a result of the French who were determined to seize whatever they could. The First World War of 1914-18 in which 14,000,000 men were killed, and 28,000,000 permanently incapacitated, is eloquent of the white man's savage competitive life. The Second World War of 1939-45 is yet another good example. During this war the holocaust was 28,000,000 and the permanently disabled more than 30,000,000. The Anglo-French wars in India and North America, the American Revolutionary War of 1776, the American-Spanish War of 1846, and a chain of others, are illustrious examples of how the white people have also been conditioned by centuries of 'savage competitive life'. The existence of British, French, Portuguese, Belgian, and Spanish colonies in and outside Africa supports our contention. Whatever they desired they seized regardless of the enormous cost in human life, not to speak of money or property.

That we may not appear to be personally manufacturing charges of European blatant savage competition, we propose quoting from some outstanding European authors. Arnold Toynbee says:

'The wholesale extermination of the previously established population, which has distinguished our English method of overseas settlement from the method of overseas settlement practised by most other Western-European peoples in modern times, is a trait which likewise distinguished the settlement of the English on the territories of the Roman Empire from the settlement of other Barbarians during the interregnum which followed the break-up of the Empire, and the dissolution of the Hellenic Society.'[1]

[1] *A Study of History* (Oxford, 1935), vol. 1, p. 465.

On the island of Tasmania the British succeeded in wiping out the entire native population in seventy-three years. Brewton Berry reports as follows:

'The [British] colonists regarded the Aborigines as a degenerate race, not so much human beings as wild beasts to be ruthlessly exterminated. Even more barbarous in their treatment of the natives were the bushrangers, convicts who had escaped into the bush where they lived a life of brigandage. These outlaws hunted the blacks for sport. They stole their women, chaining them up, outraging them, and in the end killing them. One . . . used regularly to hunt natives in order to provide his dogs with meat.

'The Aborigines, though naturally disposed towards peace and friendship with the whites, were aroused to fury by these outrages, and retaliated in kind.'[1]

The Spaniards and the Portuguese were also not exceptions, although they placed religion above race. In Brazil, for instance, the Portuguese planted in the Indian villages clothing taken from recent victims of smallpox. As the Indians were strangers to this malady they quickly succumbed.[2] Toynbee observes:

'The sense of religious solidarity and fraternity did not, however, restrain the Spaniards and the Portuguese in South America, a century and a half ago, from cold-bloodedly and brutally destroying—out of sheer greed for (non-existent) gold and for (to them, unutilizable) land—the wonderful society which had been conjured into existence by the genius of the Jesuit Missionaries, among the primitive peoples of Paraguay.'[3]

We are anxious, however, in the interest of objectivity, not to create the wrong impression that this vein of ruthlessness is the monopoly of the European peoples. The Russians, Japanese, Chinese, Indians, and Africans all share alike this 'savage competitive life' which has conditioned the entire human race, of which Cloete is part, for centuries extending beyond human memory. Our main contention is that Cloete is wrong in confining a universal truth exclusively to the Africans. It is wrong

[1] *Race Relations* (Boston: The Riverside Press Co.), p. 202, as quoted therein.
[2] Berry, op. cit., p. 204.
[3] Op. cit., p. 225, footnote 1.

logic. We are reminded of Oliver Goldsmith's essay on *National Prejudice*:

'Among a multiplicity of other topics, we took occasion to talk of the different characters of the several nations of Europe; when one of the gentlemen, cocking his hat, and assuming such an air of importance as if he had all the merit of the English nation in his own person, declared that the Dutch were a parcel of avaricious wretches; that the Germans were drunken sots, and beastly gluttons; and the Spaniards proud, haughty, and surly tyrants; but that in bravery, generosity, clemency, and in every other virtue the English excelled all the rest of the world.'

We shall now be able to put right Cloete's remark and state it thus:

'Man (European, African and Asiatic) has been conditioned by centuries of savage competitive life to seize what he desires wherever he can find it.'

The League of Nations came into existence after the First World War in order to prevent this 'savage competitive life' more especially on the part of the so-called great, civilized powers. The United Nations Organization which came into existence after the Second World War is yet another effort in that direction. We shall not belabour this point any further. We want to proceed with our examination of other Cloeteisms.

Cloete maintains that cruelty does not mean anything to the African, and that human life to him has no great value, particularly the life of a stranger.[1] Perhaps our knowledge of African philology here may help us to show that Cloete is wrong. We offer the following list for the benefit of the reader:

English	cruelty	kindness	mercy
Zulu	*isihluku*	*umusa*	*isihau*
Shona	*hasha*	*mkowa*	*mkowa*
Swahili	*ukatili*	*wema*	*rehema*
Luganda	*obukambwe*	*ekisa*	*okusasira*
Yoruba	*ika*	*iseun*	*anu*
Sotho	*sehloho*	*mofuta*	*mohau*

[1] Op. cit., p. 378.

Tswana	*borumolano*	*bopelonomi*	*bopelotlhomogi*
Lamba	*ulukansa*	*uluse*	*inkumbu*
Hausa	*kuttu*	*alheri*	*rahama*
Lomongo	*lilenga*	*liota*	*isei*

Kindness and mercy were not grafted on the African by the white man, and this is philologically demonstrated by the above list. I am at this point reminded of an incident during my school-days in Southern Rhodesia. Our British teacher was sarcastically satirizing the African people. He accused them of laziness, lies, immorality, cruelty, hatred, and a host of other vices that have escaped my memory. To impress his African students with the vices of their people he wrote these on the blackboard. The list went beyond thirty. A 12-year-old African boy who had never travelled forty miles beyond his village burst out in annoyance. 'Sir,' he said, 'what you tell us is also true of your people. You are able to tell us our evils *in the English language*. English people must have the same.'

We do not deny the African is cruel but we contend that he is not the only one. Both mercy and cruelty are well distributed among the African people just as they are among white people. What is wrong with Cloete's statement is his particularizing that which is truly universal. He speaks of cruelty as if it were exclusively an African invention.

Church history affords us countless examples of the cruelty of the peoples of Europe, but we must not be understood to attribute this cruelty exclusively to the European peoples. Far from it. We merely want to show that cruelty is not an African monopoly. The first three centuries of the Christian Church saw thousands of European Christians cruelly put to death by European rulers. Burning was their favourite sport. Cruel per-secutions under Nero (A.D. 64), Decius (A.D. 249-51), Valerian (A.D. 253-60), and Diocletian (A.D. 303-5) are well known to all readers of Church history. The struggle for power between the papacy and the state is full of many bitter, cruel religious wars which paid no regard to the worth of human life. In England the Lollards were subject to burnings and at the height of English cruelty the bones of Wycliff, their leader who had died in 1384, were dug up in 1428 and burned and the ashes thrown into a near-by stream. This point becomes more interesting when it is remembered that as recently as 1920 angry whites in the State of Nebraska, U.S.A., rushed upon a Negro who had been convicted of assaulting a white woman and seized him from the hands of the law, and beat and tied him to a stake and burned him to ashes. The burning at the stake of John Huss, Cranmer, and other European reform leaders is well known. The notorious Spanish Inquisition, the historic Massacre of Vassy in which thousands of French people lost their lives, the cruel religious wars of England beginning from the death of Henry VIII to the Glorious Revolution of 1688, and the cruel, bitter, un-Christian religious wars of American colonists of the seventeenth century are but good examples of the even distribution of cruelty over the whole race of mankind.

Cloete's assertion that the African does not care about the life of a stranger is equally incorrect. A stranger in most parts of Africa is entitled to extra protection. When David Livingstone died at Chitanda's village in Central Africa he was carried to the nearest port by the Africans 'so that he might not sleep among strangers but among his own people'. Those of us who have lived in Africa are under the impression that it is the white man who does not care for the lives of the non-whites. Indians, Japanese, Chinese, and American Negroes give the same witness. When peaceful Indian demonstrators appeared before the British headquarters in India the British General Dyer opened fire on them and killed more than 500 people. When the Hova nationalists of Madagascar demanded self-determination in 1947 France killed 80,000 of them. It is common knowledge that Germany killed 6,000,000 Jews in gas-chambers and by other methods. The notorious Nazi genocidal methods are too well known to require description. The American atomic bomb that was dropped on Hiroshima in 1945 is eloquent enough to need no comment. The existence of the Ku-Klux-Klan, whose membership consists of anything from the low-type white people to ministers of the Christian faith, and which is dedicated to the perpetration of deeds of cruelty against the Negro, clearly shows how little some of the whites in the United States value the lives of the Negroes. The historical persecution of all minority groups in the U.S.A. and Europe shows very little humanity on the part of the persecutors. This should be enough to convince our reader that when Cloete says, 'Human life to him [the African] has no great value, particularly the life of a stranger', he is guilty of erroneously attributing 'man's inhumanity to man' exclusively to the African peoples. Like all other human vices 'man's inhumanity to man' is evenly distributed over all the species of mankind. No particular race should ever deceive itself that it was specially exempted from this human weakness that has been with us since the dawn of the human race. The so-called most highly civilized nations of the earth have committed the same heinous crimes as the most primitive peoples of the earth. Newspapers are full of cases of wife-beaters, wife-killers, rape, adultery, burglary, theft, poisoning, divorce, incest, felony, and the like, in the Americas, Europe, Asia, Australasia, and Africa. Dr. Eugene A. Nida shows real insight when he says, 'Fundamentally human behaviour is very similar, and in a real sense we are all brothers under the skin'.[1]

We must close this chapter with a few observations. Writers on Africa, of the kind we have mentioned, take the well-known weaknesses and failures of mankind from the North to the South Pole, and from East to West, and heap these on the continent of Africa so that they can say to the rest of the world, 'Look at those cruel savages, who cannot appreciate the deep humanity in the New Testament, who are only inspired by the bloodshed of the Old Testament and whose centuries-long history is nothing else but a record of ruthless tribal wars. They deserve no freedom. The world is not safe in their hands.' In this way these writers hope to see white supremacy maintained everywhere in Africa. Above everything else, they show that they lack lamentably a fundamental understanding of the true nature of man. In this era when peoples of different races find themselves thrown together, living side by side with one another, it serves no good purpose whatever to distort so seriously the true picture of any one race.

[1] *Customs and Cultures*, p. 30.

Since men and women of good will are working to bring about understanding and peace in a world whose only legacy now seems to be tension, insecurity, and fear, it is necessary that subjectiveness be put aside in the interest of getting down to the truth—the objective truth which cannot fail to bring us down on our knees so that, with contrite hearts, we may recognize that through the whole human race runs a strong vein of ruthlessness, savagery, cruelty, weakness, and frailty. It is this comprehensive truth that will make the black man, the white man, the yellow man, and the brown man realize that we all have gone astray like lost sheep, and we all stand in great need of redemption through divine action.

CHAPTER TEN

The Majority Mind of Europeans

The European in Africa finds himself surrounded by many enemies of his own making. This arises out of his unwillingness to share equal citizenship with people outside his racial group. This is another way of saying that the white man's determination to impose his will on Africa, regardless of what the Africans feel, has created a situation in which the white man finds himself surrounded by fires which could be extinguished easily if only he took the right attitude towards other people outside his own race. In a sense the white man finds himself between two big fires. On the one hand he fears the march and triumph of democracy in Africa since this implies the annihilation of white supremacy to which he clings so dearly. He fears the success of that for which he has stood for centuries! On the other hand, the white man fears the possible rise of communism in Africa since democracy and communism can never dwell under the same roof. The triumph of one is the defeat of the other. With one hand the white man in Africa seems to be saying, 'Keep communism out of Africa', and with the other he seems to be saying, 'Keep democracy away from Africans'.

But fate seems to have sealed the doom of white supremacy since, if communism or democracy became an accomplished fact on the continent of Africa, white supremacy would have no leg on which to stand. Viewed from this angle therefore we see democracy and communism forming an unholy alliance which will explode white supremacy. But added to this unholy pact is African nationalism which strengthens the hands of democracy to the detriment of white supremacy; and it cannot be denied altogether that African nationalism can use communism as an instrument with which to procure African freedom and independence, just as American colonists used French weapons to get their independence without necessarily going French. In practical terms the situation in Africa boils down to this: The white man fears communism which threatens his way of life: he fears democracy since it is based on the will of the majority, and in this case the majority are the Africans whom the white man would exclude from any participation in the central government of the country; he fears nationalism since it demands the extension of democracy to the majority of the people who happen to be non-white. It is at this point that the honest thinking of the white man in Africa breaks down so that he is torn between the voice of right and might, the scales tipping discernibly to the latter. But he is scared to listen wholly to the latter since that would be a reversion to the law of the jungle whereby the weakest animal is at the mercy of the strongest. It was Aneurin Bevan who once warned during the Anglo-French military invasion of Egypt, 'If the government wants to reimpose the law of the jungle, they must remember that Britain and France are not the most powerful animals in it. There are much more dangerous animals prowling around.'

This ambivalence on the part of the European in Africa has produced what we call, for want of a better word, a split mind, a mind that subtly and openly defies the ordinary moral laws when it comes to matters that affect the freedom and the independence of the African people. The European in Africa, though he claims to be a champion of democracy, is, in his actions, democracy's worst enemy since he is determined, by hook or by crook, to see that democracy is not extended to the millions of Africans who are actually demanding it. It seems reasonable to postulate that if democracy is only reserved for Europeans, then the teeming millions of Africans must find something else in its place. However disagreeable the memory of Mau Mau terrorism, an objective student cannot help being impressed by the fact that the whole movement was one of desperation seeking the recognition of the legitimate claims of the African people. The Mau Mau members resorted to these desperate measures because they wanted a say in the affairs of their country. This fact is supported by many Kenya Africans with whom we have had occasion to discuss the matter, and also by the fact that during and after Mau Mau terrorism some political reforms with a semblance of

African participation in the central government of the country were introduced. The Mau Mau movement shook the British out of their political complacency and this has been to the good, though at a terrible cost of human life.

France affords another good example of how European powers will move heaven and earth to see that democracy in Africa remains the white man's monopoly. The French policy towards Africans who demand self-government, until recently at any rate, is one of brutal repression, flat refusal to grant Africans freedom and full independence. In Morocco, for instance, when the Arabs demanded their full independence, the French deposed the rightful Sultan Mohammed V and replaced him with their puppet Sultan Ben Arafa. The difference between the two Sultans was that Mohammed V resisted the imposition of the French people upon the Arabs, whereas Ben Arafa supported the French imposition. In answer to this act the Moroccans massacred over 2,000 French *colons*, and in retaliation the French Army and Air Force destroyed whole tribes and villages. It is believed that 60,000 Arabs were killed. All this was done so as to fulfil the French prayer, 'The will of the French people shall be done in Morocco as it is in France'. But the Moroccans were equally determined—'The will of the Moroccans, and not of the French, shall be done in Morocco'. With the return of Mohammed V to Morocco and the granting of full independence to the Moroccans, peace and order returned to this part of Africa.

Algeria was the next to demand full independence from France, and the same brutal repression greeted her. It is estimated that there are now (1957) more than 300,000 French troops ready to fight the Algerian rebels. It is calculated by French military experts that if this number could be increased to 400,000, the whole Algerian revolt would be wiped out. In simple language, because the Algerians demand full independence they must be wiped out, and leave only those who submit to the will of the French. It is really a contest in which either the French or the Arab will dominate in the affairs of Algeria as a whole. To many African observers the Russian brutality during the Hungarian Revolt cannot surpass that of France in the Algerian

Revolt. The Algerian Revolt, like the Hungarian Revolt, is really an effort on the part of the Algerians to have democracy. Incidentally, here we see that an African who aspires to democracy is as much an object of European hatred and suspicions as one who tries to embrace communism. An African democrat, or communist, or nationalist, is a target for French bullets. In short the French aim at making the Algerians count for nothing, but the Algerians resist this 'nothing-fication' of the Algerian people.

We have stated in the last chapter that democracy is the 'will of the majority'. The essence of communism or dictatorship is just the reverse—'the will of the minority'. Democracy as practised in Britain, Western Europe, and the U.S.A. accords roughly with the classical definition, but democracy as practised by European powers in Africa agrees with the standard definition of communism or dictatorship, since in European-ruled Africa it is not the will of the African majority that counts, but that of a European minority. While in Europe they have Russian communism, which threatens Western democracy, in Africa we are confronted with European dictatorship which threatens African *kuzwitonga* or *ukuzibusa* (self-determination). In brief, democracy as practised by Europeans in Africa is neither European nor African. It is much closer to Russian communism since European powers owe their existence in Africa to military force and not to the will of the majority. The majority of the people on the continent of Africa are at their mercy just as the communist satellite countries of Europe are at the mercy of Russian communism. The people have no constitutional means of overthrowing any white government that mismanages their affairs. Surely, for 150,000,000 Africans to be at the mercy of 5,000,000 whites could not be said to be African or European democracy in the best sense of the word? The arrow clearly points in the direction of communism.

In dealing with one another, Europeans follow democratic methods, but in their dealings with the African they adopt communistic or dictatorial methods. Democracy for themselves, and dictatorship for Africans! There was never a better example of a double standard. This is what we mean by the European 'split mind'—a mind that pursues two radically opposite political ideologies.

In the rest of this chapter our main task is to endeavour to interpret the European mind with regard to the question of African freedom and independence so that the reader may see clearly what is involved in the nationalistic struggle going on in Africa. We are aware, however, that we are now treading on slippery ground since an interpretation is not infallible, and since it is difficult to know what So-and-So meant when he made such-and-such a statement. Our line of interpretation will there-fore follow that of describing and explaining the impressions made on the African mind by political pronouncements made by leading Europeans. We propose taking even the most important men and laying them on our political operation table, and con-ducting a thorough surgical examination, since what they say and do greatly affect the body politic of multiracial Africa. Like the surgeon's knife, which cuts the poor and the rich alike to discover what is inside the patient, our political knife will do precisely the same thing in the interest of multiracial Africa.

It was Sir Winston Churchill who once said that he did not become Prime Minister of Britain in order to preside over the liquidation of His Majesty's Empire. This was said at the time India was demanding full independence from Britain. To the Africans that meant only one thing: that Sir Winston Churchill was determined to perpetuate British imperialism, and this meant the perpetuation of African subjection. It meant the denial of African freedom and independence. Many an African just won-dered how it was that the same man who opposed Nazi domina-tion could make a statement that purported the very thing against which he was so heroically standing. It became clear to the Africans that, while Sir Winston Churchill had championed the cause of Western democracy, he was unwilling to extend the same democracy to the colonial peoples. To the Africans it sounded like, 'Freedom for the British, and subjection for the African', since the granting of freedom to the African or any other peoples subjected by the British necessarily meant the liquidation of the British Empire, which liquidation Sir Winston

Churchill was anxious to avoid. It is this apparent double standard which baffles many an African in his attempt to understand Western peoples.

Albert Schweitzer, who has done so much for thousands of African people in his lifetime, also forms a rewarding study of European attitudes towards the African people. John Gunther gives Albert Schweitzer's attitude towards the African people in the following words:

'The idea of the rights of man was formed and developed . . . when society was an organized and stable thing. . . . In a disordered society the very well-being of man himself often demands that his fundamental rights be abridged.'[1]

The impression this makes on the African mind is that Schweitzer is averse to full African independence. He appears to assume that there was never such a thing as organized and stable African society and that there was never such a thing as the right of man in an African society. In other words the idea of the right of man is non-African. Schweitzer seems to assume that African society was always disordered. If this is what Schweitzer means, there can be nothing farther from the truth. Although African society is so simple and primitive, it has amazing organization and stability which students of African anthropology readily concede. The genius of European rule in Africa lies in their indirect rule which is based on the recognition of the social organization and stability of various African tribes. Indirect rule merely means the imposition of the rule of a strong military power over an organized stable tribe or group of tribes who have a weak military system. Indirect rule does not create a new order, but rather manipulates, exploits and utilizes to the full extent the pattern of life it finds among the natives themselves. If, therefore, Schweitzer means that the African society was disorganized and unstable, facts have proved the contrary.

From this erroneous assumption of a disordered society, Schweitzer advances his argument of abridging some of the fundamental human rights in so far as these affect the African. In the African mind, Schweitzer's reasoning seems to run along

[1] *Inside Africa*, p. 37.

these lines. African society is disordered. Full human rights can only be exercised properly in a well-ordered society. Therefore, since African society is so disordered, African human rights must be abridged.

The African is keenly interested in determining the real meaning of abridging some of these fundamental human rights. One African student from Tanganyika rendered Schweitzer's statement as follows:

'Schweitzer is simply telling the world this: "The fundamental human rights of the African must be abridged. Don't give him all the fundamental human rights because he belongs to a disordered society. The world may be greatly endangered if you do so." In short, Schweitzer is saying: "Don't give the African full freedom and full independence."'

This interpretation of Schweitzer may look somewhat exaggerated, and so we shall attempt a justification for it. The African looks around him to see the practical implications of this theory of abridging fundamental human rights, and he is more and more impressed by what he sees meted out against him by the European powers. He observes that many times when African workers go on strike the government declares a state of emergency, thus placing the African leaders at the mercy of the law. But in the case of European strikes no such emergency measures are taken. The African further notes that when African political organizations fight tooth and nail against discriminatory legislation, the government, which is usually white, passes laws that almost neutralize such organizations. While the government recognizes the legitimate existence of such an organization it deliberately cripples its activities. The African notes that whenever the Africans demand their freedom, which is their birthright, the leaders of such freedom-movements are quickly arrested, and Schweitzer's meaning of abridging fundamental human rights becomes very clear to the African.

We may now ask ourselves: What does abridging fundamental human rights mean? Obviously, the statement does not mean total deprivation, or absolute denial of rights. It means partial deprivation or partial denial of these rights. This, in turn, means partial recognition, or partial affirmation. To abridge the fundamental rights of man is to take away some of these rights but to leave others, both the quality and quantity of which are determined by the one who chooses to abridge them. What are these human rights? Equality of human beings in dignity and rights; freedom from discrimination on the ground of race, colour, sex, language, religion, and political creeds; and freedom of speech, expression, enterprise, and the press. Freedom of self-determination of all peoples is one of these fundamental human rights.

It is clear then that to abridge any of these rights is to interfere with these fundamental human rights. In the final analysis, to accept this doctrine of abridging these rights, is to place one group of people at the mercy of another. In plain language, to abridge African human rights is to place the African people at the mercy of the European powers. If this be acceptable, it would mean that the African derives his human rights from these European powers. It would mean that these European powers are the chief source of the fundamental human rights of the African when actually the African derives his human rights, not from the fact that he belongs to this or that European power, but from the fact that he belongs to the human family. It is obvious, therefore, that the abridger of fundamental human rights is, by all standards of good logic, a dictator—the very antithesis of democracy.

Perhaps Slobodan M. Draskovich has a point which is very helpful at this juncture. In his brilliant analysis of the nature of communism he observes: '. . . the right of peoples to freedom, independence and self-determination is recognized only if and when it serves the interests of the communist revolution and consolidation of communist power.'[1] He might as well have said: 'The communists abridge fundamental human rights where their interests are threatened.' This becomes even more pertinent when it is remembered that the abridger is the white man who has vital interests on the continent of Africa.

It was Joseph Stalin who once said:
'There are occasions when the right of self-determination conflicts with . . . higher right—the right of the working class that

[1] Slobodan M. Draskovich: *Tito, Moscow's Trojan Horse*, pp. 32–3.

has assumed power to consolidate its power. In such cases—this must be said bluntly—the right to self-determination cannot and must not serve as an obstacle to the exercise by the working class of its right to dictatorship. The former must give way to the latter. That, for instance, was the case in 1920, when in order to defend the power of the working class, we were obliged to march on Warsaw.'

Clearly communism purports, not to deny altogether fundamental human rights, but to abridge them. In motivation and goal Joseph Stalin stood for no more and for no less than the European powers stand for in Africa. The French imperialist might as well have said:

'There are occasions when the African right of self-determination conflicts with . . . higher right—the right of the French government that has assumed power to consolidate its power. In such cases—this must be said bluntly—the African right to self-determination cannot and must not serve as an obstacle to the exercise by the French government of its right to sovereignty. The former must give way to the latter. That, for instance, was the case in 1957, when in order to defend the French rule, we were obliged to march on Algeria.'

Another interesting aspect of Schweitzer's thinking is his 'elder brother' theory in African-European relations. He says:

'A word about the relations of the whites and the blacks. What must be the general character of the intercourse between them? Am I to treat the black man as my equal or my inferior? I must show him that I can respect the dignity of human personality in everyone, and this attitude in me he must be able to see for himself; but the essential thing is that there shall be real brotherliness. How far this is to find complete expression in the sayings and doings of daily life must be settled by circumstances. The Negro is a child, and with children nothing can be done without the use of authority. We must, therefore, so arrange the circumstances of daily life that my natural authority can find expression. With regard to the Negroes, then, I have coined the formula: "I am your brother, it is true, but your elder brother." '[1]

[1] Charles R. Joy: *Albert Schweitzer: An Anthology*, p. 85.

Schweitzer (like the Dutch who regarded Indonesians as innocent little children who needed at all times Dutch paternal care) regards the African as a child. He plays the common role of the big 'white father', and if there is any blunder that most white people commit this is surely one. This reminds me of a conversation I had one day with a white student. 'You see, Sithole, we don't like Nasser', he said.

'Why don't you?' I asked him.

'Because he's more inclined towards Russia', said he, as if inclination towards Russia and disinclination from the West merited death itself.

'Well,' said I, 'what else could he do? He wanted to buy arms from the Western powers, and he was carefully controlled as to what to buy.'

'But, you see,' he said, 'selling arms to Egypt would be like selling arms to a child, and you know what happens when arms are in the hands of children.'

'That's exactly the reason why Nasser has turned to Russia. We all like to deal with those who treat us like men, not with those who treat us like little children.'

This attitude of treating all non-Westerners like children is prevalent among Westerners. The Dutch were surprised when the Indonesians, whom they had treated all along like little children, led a successful revolution which ended in the freedom and full independence of more than 78,000,000 Indonesians. The African interpretation of Schweitzer's regarding the African as a child is correct—namely, that Schweitzer deliberately reduces an adult African to a child so that he can justify the superimposition of European authority on the African. It is an insult for one man to regard another man as a child. This attitude of Schweitzer is even more clearly shown in his 'elder brother' theory.

Schweitzer admits the fact that the black man and the white man are brothers, but he qualifies this by saying that the white man is the black man's elder brother. The concept of elder brother is inconceivable in the absence of a younger brother. In this case, therefore, the black man is the younger brother of the white man. In African society the elder brother is looked up to by the younger brother in this life and the life to come. The African construes Schweitzer's elder brother theory only in this sense. In other words, the elder brother, according to African custom, holds sway over his younger brother indefinitely. In politics, therefore, the elder brother theory means domination of the Africans (younger brother) by whites (elder brother). The African sees in this theory not temporary but permanent domination of the African people, since, chronologically, the younger brother never can catch up with the elder brother. This means white domination and African subjection in perpetuity. While Schweitzer's acceptance of the concept of brotherliness between black and white commends itself to the heart of the African, yet its elder brother aspect strikes deep fear in the heart of the African. It suggests very strongly to the African that at the back of Schweitzer's mind is indefinite African subjection. His three theories—namely, abridging some of the fundamental human rights of the African, that the Negro is a child and therefore the white man is his father, and that the white man is the black man's elder brother—strongly support the common view among the African thinkers that, fundamentally, Schweitzer is opposed to racial equality in any form. This view of Schweitzer's is, moreover, shared by many white people.

An examination of the various political doctrines prevalent in Africa will show clearly how the European mind works in relation to the African people. In British East Africa, for instance, a new type of government policy is being hammered out, and this is the so-called multiracialism. The avowed intention of this policy is that all races in a multiracial society shall participate fully in the central government of the country. In other words, multiracialism is an effort to do away with the already unacceptable exclusive European policy, and an effort to bring about an inclusive policy. The argument against an exclusively white government and in favour of an inclusive policy is that a multiracial society should be reflected in the multiracial composition of the government. This is to say that only a multiracial government can truly reflect a healthy multiracial society. In accordance with this doctrine, therefore, the principle of direct racial representation has been fully accepted and implemented. Although this policy has its glaring shortcomings it is definitely an advance on the previous policy which excluded the African from any participation in the government of the country.

On the other hand, however, a closer examination of this policy reveals that politics in multiracial British East Africa run on racial tracks, and that its real intention is to bypass adult universal suffrage in the sole interest of white supremacy. In Kenya, for example, in the Legislative Council, there are 14 Europeans, 14 Africans, 6 Asians and 1 Arab who make up the unofficial members. The gist of this multiracial set-up is that the number of non-white members shall not exceed that of the whites. Out of 32 official members there is provision for only 2 African members, so that in the entire Legislative Council of 67 members (32 official and 35 unofficial members) there are only 14 Africans who represent 5,000,000 Africans whereas the non-African members represent less than a quarter of a million non-Africans (whites and A iatics). Tanganyika, which has a 10-10-10 parity (whites, Africans and Asiatics), shows the same political trend, i.e. 10 Africans represent 7,000,000 Africans whereas the rest represent less than a quarter of a million people. Multi-racialism accords to all races a say in the government of the country but it also clearly shows serious defects as a permanent solution to the present problems.

While multiracialism allows group participation, and recognizes group rights, it denies individual citizenship rights. Multiracialism as practised in British East Africa means that other races are allowed to participate in governmental affairs so long as they are satisfied with a secondary place in the whole scheme, while the first place is reserved for whites only. In the final analysis multiracialism as an instrument of government is a subtle entrenchment of white supremacy, a domination of one race by another, a rule by minority and not by majority, and a refusal to create a common electorate. This is the fatal weakness of multiracialism. It is a political solution based on the principle of ignoring the legitimate claims of the majority of the people in favour of those of a minority.

The Kenya settlers put it more openly when they said:

'We are opposed to any scheme of provincial independence which might go so far as to deprive Europeans of leadership and control of the colony as a whole.'[1]

At the bottom of multiracialism we see European autocracy at work, and it is this that often puzzles the African when he is called upon to distinguish between Russian communists and European powers in Africa. These two seem to be blood-brothers. They are both for ever seeking domination of other people. With both of them the will of the majority does not count, but only that of a minority. To refuse adult universal franchise is to refuse the granting of some of the basic human rights to the majority of the people. The triumph of multiracialism, therefore, if it remained as it is at present, would be the triumph of white supremacy and the perpetuation of African subjection.

In the Federation of Rhodesia and Nyasaland we find another policy by a different name, but fundamentally the same as multiracialism. This is the policy of partnership. The principle of direct African representation has been accepted and implemented. According to the federal constitution of Rhodesia and Nyasaland only twelve Africans represent 6,500,000 Africans and the rest (except for three Europeans specially elected to represent African interests) represent less than 300,000 whites.

When the Federation was pressed to define the meaning of partnership, the white politicians found it expedient to do this in terms of senior and junior partners—the former being the whites, and the latter, of course, Africans. But when more political pressure was exerted, the government came out with a bolder statement that 'the government must remain in the hands of civilized and responsible people'. This was as good as saying that, at least for the present, 'racial equality will bring about black domination over whites, and this must be resisted'. Such a construction is justified by the fact that this standard of civilization and responsibility can only be determined by the white man himself who is unwilling to abdicate power over Africa. It is clear then that even in the Federation of Rhodesia and Nyasaland,

[1] *Africa South*, vol. 1, no. 3, April–June 1957, p. 73.

whose policy is midway between the apartheid policy of the
Union of South Africa and that of adult universal franchise, we
find entrenched deeply the desire to maintain white ascendancy
over the black man.

It was Cecil John Rhodes who coined the dictum, 'Equal
rights for all civilized men' in reference to British-occupied
Africa. This dictum, as it did not promise to give these rights
immediately to the African, was easily accepted by Europeans
because at that time there was hardly any African who possessed
sufficient externals of Western civilization. But today the situation is different, and the white man, in view of the present large
number of 'civilized' Africans, is confronted with redeeming or
dishonouring his promise. The idea of equal citizenship with the
African is to him abhorrent. And so the European finds himself
engaging in a faith-shaking occupation of manufacturing countless ingenious definitions of 'civilized' so that he can exclude, with
a semblance of legality, most eligible Africans from qualifying as
registered voters. The political battle raging in British East Africa
and the Federation of Rhodesia and Nyasaland is one of forestalling the creation of adult universal franchise in favour of
racial group participation. Bluntly stated, the white man insists
on being the first citizen of Africa. The African also wants to be
one, and anything less than this is unacceptable since it involves
being discriminated against. 'Racial discrimination', to borrow
the Rev. George Gay's words, 'has no meaning apart from
degradation.' It is this European-inflicted stigma which the
African now seeks to remove. While the African accepts multiracialism or partnership, he views this as an interim measure
because both policies have a tendency to perpetuate this European-
inflicted stigma which has subjected the African to the ridicule
of the rest of mankind. Dr. Kwame Nkrumah is right when he
says:

'I saw that the whole solution to this problem lay in political
freedom for our people, for it is only when a people are politically
free that other races can give them the respect that is due to them.
It is impossible to talk of equality of races in any other terms. No
people without a government of their own can expect to be

treated on the same level as peoples of independent sovereign states. . . . No race, no people, no nation can exist freely and be respected at home and abroad without political freedom.'[1]

It was Mr. Wellington Chirwa, M.P., sensing the real implications of the Federation which was imposed on Nyasaland, who openly stated:

'It is the duty of every African in this country [Nyasaland] to see that federation is broken up so that Nyasaland should attain its full self-determination. . . . As far as I am concerned, the right to rule this country belongs to the African people to whom it rightly belongs, and any attempt to entrench power in the hands of Europeans by any franchise system will inevitably fail and lead the country to great disaster and bitterness.'[2]

Mr. Chirwa has his finger on the real tension spot within the Federation of Rhodesia and Nyasaland. Who has the right to rule the country? Is it the majority or the minority? Is it the rightful owners of the country, or a group of people who claim to be civilized and responsible? Apparently, the policy of the Federation of Rhodesia and Nyasaland has transferred the people's right to rule to a group of people who call themselves civilized and responsible and this is the folly of the Federal policy—it is based on the will of the minority and not that of the majority. The people's rights are overridden by the claims of those who claim to be civilized and responsible.

The same question was taken up by Mr. Zuberi M. M. Mtemvu, in a long circular letter:

'Sir Godfrey Huggins duped the British Parliament and public with the slogan "equal rights for all civilized men". To us "civilized" is less important than "men". The word "civilized" has no such significance in our political vocabulary. Our slogan is "equal rights for all men". If our non-African neighbours think they are too superior to be thus lumped together on an equality with their inferiors, that is their own business, not ours. . . .'[3]

After the Tredgold Commission of Inquiry into the franchise laws of Southern Rhodesia, two separate classes of voters were

[1] *Ghana: The Autobiography of Kwame Nkrumah*, pp. xiv–xv.
[2] *The Sunday Mail*, Salisbury, 16 June 1957, p. 2.
[3] *East Africa and Rhodesia*, 4 April 1957, p. 1041.

recommended—A and B, the former being general and the latter special voters. The former are mostly Europeans who enjoy adult universal franchise and the latter mostly Africans with very limited franchise. In short, the whole aim of this set-up is to maintain the ascendancy of A (Europeans) over B (Africans), and to ensure the subservience of B to A, that is, the domination of the African majority by a white minority. This is what Mr. Enoch Dumbutshena meant when he said:

'I expected the [Tredgold] Commission to reduce the means of qualifications so that as many people as possible could take part in the election of the members of Parliament. The division of voters into two groups of varying status is to my humble mind racial. The special voters will be Africans and the Europeans will dominate the ordinary votes. Two classes of electors—an inevitable racial division.

'If we get rid of the fear of racial domination, the fear of being one day dominated, then we shall find that nothing, in this business of democracy, is better than universal franchise.'[1]

In short, Africans want adult universal franchise but European powers are unwilling to grant this. The struggle going on on the continent of Africa is to decide whether the majority or the minority shall rule.

It was Jomo Kenyatta, the so-called brains of the Mau Mau movement, who once said, 'A white man will always seek power over the black man. It is his nature.' Events in Africa have not discredited this saying of Kenyatta. Even a superficial observation of the multiracial policy of British East Africa, and the partnership policy of the Federation of Rhodesia and Nyasaland reveals clearly that tendency of the white man for ever seeking power over the black man. If the African could submit himself to this desire most of the problems between black and white would vanish overnight. The trouble begins when the African makes a real effort to resist this European desire.

We have now shown how the African looks at the European mind in general. He seeks to understand him, but this double standard of the white man still puzzles him so that today the

[1] *Concord*, June 1957, no. 11, p. 15.

African has become extremely cautious and realistic in his dealings with the white man. Whatever political schemes the white man makes as a solution for multiracial Africa, the African will remain suspicious and distrustful of them so long as they purport to entrench white supremacy, and hence African subjection. The French system of internal autonomy for her African colonies is not the answer to the problem of African independence. Internal autonomy under over-all French rule is nothing but glorified subjection. People want to rule themselves. African sovereignty within European sovereignty is no sovereignty at all, just as American or British independence under the general supervision of Russia or China would not be true independence.

Of course, it has been pointed out that for defence purposes it is extremely important that these weak and half-developed and undeveloped African countries should be under some powerful European powers. We have discussed this matter with some outstanding European and American experts on Africa. They say African countries need Western defence, economic aid, Western skills and education, as if to say, 'Because Africa needs these things it must be European-ruled'.

No thinking African can deny that Africa very badly needs Western help, but no thinking African accepts this as justification for his being European-ruled. Rather, the thinking African puts to severe test the European thinking in this fashion. Suppose we admit that European powers are sincere in saying that for defence purposes weak African countries must be occupied by European powers, this would be giving European powers untold power over the whole continent of Africa. By this line of argument, European powers and the U.S.A. have no right to object to the occupation of European countries by Russia since these are occupied for defence purposes. It is clearly dangerous to allow a bigger power to occupy a weaker country on defence, economic, and other pretensions, the more so if this be against the wish of that weaker country.

It is obvious that the European powers are caught in a dilemma. They need to re-think the entire structure of their relations with Africa so that they may be better able to adjust their attitude to the fast-changing conditions all over Africa. While the white man lives in the latter half of the twentieth century, yet his mind, in relation to Africa, is still much closer to that of the end of the eighteenth century, and this does not help to solve the problems of the present-day multiracial Africa.

CHAPTER ELEVEN

Africa and Communism

In this chapter we want to consider the question of communism in relation to Africa. Does the African in general take readily to communism? Does he like communism as a political ideology? Does he see his own salvation in communism? In other words, does communism, from the point of view of the African himself, hold any bright prospects? It is not our intention to give any false assurances here that the African is for or against communism. We want to examine honestly the actual and possible relation of African nationalism to communism. We feel that the most effective way of doing this is to orientate the reader historically before we discuss the whole question.

Egypt affords us a good starting-point, partly because she is a sovereign African state that is so much in the news, and partly because her struggle for full independence will throw more light on our later discussion.

The British first occupied Egypt in 1882. In 1883 they promised the Egyptians that they were going to withdraw the British forces as soon as conditions would warrant such a step. The British troops were not withdrawn until 1955. In 1919 there was a serious insurrection against the British. This was led by Zaghul, the famous Egyptian patriot. In 1921 the Egyptians organized a passive resistance campaign against the British. The following year the British were forced to give Egypt limited independence. The assassination of Sir Lee Stack by a fanatical Egyptian nationalist took place in 1924 and the Egyptians felt the full blast of British vengeance. In 1936, after a hard struggle against the British, Egypt became fully independent, and in 1937 she was admitted to the League of Nations as a sovereign state. On 23 July 1952, the famous Nasser-Naguib coup finally seized all power and influence from King Farouk, the Wafd (nationalistic party), and the British. For the first time in the modern history of Egypt, ruled by foreigners for centuries, she became her own ruler.

The Egyptian struggle for freedom and independence was a bitter one. The British often placed obstacles in Egypt's way. Every time the Egyptians asked the British to quit Egypt the British refused to do so. Colonel Nasser says:

'They [the British] said they were on the point of leaving, and always found an excuse to stay. At first they claimed they were in Egypt to protect foreigners against the Egyptians, although foreigners never asked for their protection; then they claimed they had to stay to protect Christian and Jewish minorities against the Moslems, overlooking the fact that the Christians and the Jews had joined the Moslems in demanding the withdrawal of the British forces from Egypt. The defence of the Suez Canal and the maintenance of their lines of communication with India and their Far Eastern empire were further pretexts. When World War II came they said they could not go because the Suez Canal was an important base, and after World War II they explained that they had to stay to safeguard the interests of the free world.'[1]

In short, it was a miracle that Egypt ever won her full independence from Britain. For the first time in their life the Egyptians have faith in themselves as masters of their own destinies. They have learned from bitter experience what it means to be under a foreign power. It would not be too much to say that Egyptian history has conditioned Egypt against foreign rule. Perhaps this explains why the Egyptians are so sensitive about their new sovereignty. Perhaps this also explains why the Egyptians will not receive orders from Washington, D.C., London, and Moscow. They just want to rule themselves. They have had enough of being ruled by foreign powers.

The question now arises: Will Egypt exchange British imperialism for Russian communism? After almost 2,500 years of foreign domination, will Egypt exchange her new full independence and national sovereignty for Russian communism? Communism in any part of Africa has no meaning outside foreign domination. It would appear that Egyptian consciousness is permeated with real hatred of British imperialism. But this

[1] *Foreign Affairs*, January 1955.

imperialism could be exercised by any other power, so that Egypt may be said to be anti-imperialistic no matter from what source this may come. She wants to be a friend of the U.S.A. but she does not want to go too near her lest she lose her full independence. She wants to go along with London, but she dreads the return of British imperialism. She wants to go along with Moscow, but the same fear strikes deep down in her national heart. She wants to hold her own. She will take orders from no other country. This she demonstrated in the Suez Canal crisis, from the day of the nationalization of the Canal to the time of the Anglo-French military operations against her.

But, of course, it may be objected that Egypt embraces communism because she carries on considerable foreign trade with Russia, Czecho-Slovakia, and Red China. In the first place, Egypt wants to live and she will trade with any country that will make this possible. It may be said, in all fairness, that the Western economic squeeze on Egypt drove Egypt to seek markets elsewhere. The 1956 withdrawal of the Old Suez Canal Company from the Canal, for instance, sent Egypt recruiting pilots in Russia, Czecho-Slovakia, and elsewhere, not because she was necessarily communistic but because she needed service no matter from what source it came. The West seems to have pursued the mistaken policy of trying to bring Egypt down on her knees, and naturally Egypt has had to make a real effort not to allow this to happen. Perhaps we may draw an inference that if Egypt won't bow to the West, there is a fairly good chance of her not bowing to Russia. It was Nasser who said:

'There would not be any communist infiltration in any part of the Middle East and Africa if the United States could develop a courageous policy—and the only morally correct one—of supporting those who are anxious to get rid of foreign domination and exploitation. Real independence would be the greatest defence against communist—or any other type of—infiltration or aggression. Free men are the most fanatical defenders of their liberty, nor do they lightly forget those who have championed their struggle for independence.'[1]

[1] *Foreign Affairs.*

Gerald Sparrow says, in reference to Nasser's anti-communist stand:

'When Colonel Nasser says Egypt will not go communist he is quite sincere. The communist mentality, founded on envy, and enforced by police rule, makes no appeal to Egyptians.'[1]

John Gunther says about Egypt's relation to communism:

'. . . on the domestic side of the fence Egypt is rigidly, resolutely anti-communist. The communist party has, of course, been suppressed, and the authorities vigilantly seek to stamp out subterranean communist activity.'[2]

Anwar El Sadat writes with typical Egyptian pride:

'Time and experience suggest that tyranny is very close to anarchy, in that both end by destroying the values of civilization: justice, morality and reason. A state which does not care for the well-being of its people ceases to be a state, and the people have a right to act in accordance with natural law. It is their right to fight against despotism, treason or any menace to the life of the community. It is the people who set up governments, and define the limits of authority. The Egyptian leaders failed to fulfil their obligations, and their power reverted to the people. The people reclaimed their sovereignty.

'In 1952, the Egyptians did only what the English did under Cromwell three hundred years before; what the Americans did in 1776; and the French in 1789.'[3]

This is a fair sample of the present Egyptian thinking and sentiment. They see themselves in the light of the English, Americans, and French who won their independence and kept it for themselves, down to this day. It is hard to imagine how the proud, independent Egyptians who have successfully thrown off the British yoke can now prepare their necks to have Russia place her yoke on them.

Now we turn to North Africa. We begin with Morocco. The Moroccan Empire, which lasted for nearly 1,200 years, was founded in A.D. 788. The French established their power in

[1] *The Sphinx Awakes*, p. 135, footnote.
[2] *Inside Africa*, p. 216.
[3] *Revolt on the Nile*, p. 136.

Morocco in 1902. While they maintained that their occupation of Morocco was in reality to protect, and not to subject, an independent power, nevertheless they held the substance of power. Morocco was under French martial law from 1914 (two years after the French had legally established their protective authority) to 1955 when Morocco, through the direct intervention of the United Nations, became a sovereign independent state.

The Moroccan struggle for full independence was epitomized in the nationalist movement called the Istiqlal, founded in 1943. Though there had been other nationalist movements prior to this date, nevertheless it is this Istiqlal that was of consequence in the liberation of Morocco. In 1947 the then Sultan of Morocco demanded full rights for Morocco as a protectorate. He had the backing of the Istiqlal. In 1950 he visited Paris for the same purpose. There was general tension throughout the country. In February 1951, Marshal Juin demanded of the Sultan that he sign a statement denouncing the Istiqlal and promised him deposition if he refused to sign. A compromise of some kind was reached between him and the Sultan. In 1952, the Sultan, delivering the usually moderate and French-thanking annual speech from the Throne, hinted that the country must get rid of its 'baby clothes'. This naturally displeased the French but pleased the nationalists.

In December 1952, there were serious riots in Casablanca. The French authorities moved like lightning and outlawed the Istiqlal, on whose support the Sultan leaned heavily. In August 1953, there were further nationalist riots in Oujda, Casablanca, and other centres. Again the French acted with their usual dramatic swiftness. The Sultan (Mohammed V) was deposed, and without much ado flown to Corsica where the world-shaking Buonaparte, who once dominated Europe, was born. Believing that Corsica was too close to Morocco for their comfort, the Sultan was flown on 25 January 1954 to the island of Madagascar. Arafa, the French-chosen Sultan, was then enthroned, but with much more limited authority than Mohammed V had hitherto been allowed to exercise.

But the Istiqlal, though outlawed and deprived of a powerful figure such as Mohammed V, did not despair. Political assassinations became rife. The Istiqlal contended that Morocco had no national elections, that it had no civil liberties, i.e. no freedom of the press, speech, or of assembly; that the French deliberately starved the Moroccans of education, and that the French were determined to prevent the unionization of Moroccan labour. But above all, the fact of being, and the thought of remaining, a subject people, greatly disturbed them. One Moroccan was reported as saying, 'We shall create a hell here until we get our independence'. There was no peace and order in Morocco until Mohammed V was reinstated and Morocco granted her independence in 1955.

In Tunisia, the same story can be told, as it can in other independent African states. But we shall not go into these since, with the exception of Liberia, the national struggle for independence has the same motivation, though methods may differ. This point, however, must be made clear, that an African nationalist movement is an honest effort on the part of the African people to reassert their human dignity which the foreign powers have denied them. It is an honest effort to overthrow foreign rule that relegates them to an inferior position.

What then is the significance of these facts in our consideration of the relation between African nationalism and Russian communism? Let it be remembered right from the beginning that while, at present, subject African peoples seem to be directing their minds against British, French, and other European rule, yet in reality they are directing their minds against foreign rule. It is not so much British or French rule that the African dislikes, as foreign rule. That the rule happens to be British or French is purely accidental. The struggle going on in Africa is against foreign domination. The British and the French happen to be the practical expression of that foreign rule. When the British and the French cease to be the embodiment of foreign rule, the struggle against them automatically ceases. By way of contrast, there is at present no such intense struggle between Russia and Africa as there is between Africa and the various European powers occupying Africa. The reason is not far to seek.

Russia does not represent, in the eyes of the African, foreign rule, whereas the European powers are the practical expression of that rule.

The overthrow of Italian rule in Ethiopia, that of the British in Egypt and the then Gold Coast, and that of the French in Morocco and Tunisia, represent the successful ejection of foreign rule from these countries. Any other rule from outside these countries could be just as good, or just as bad, as the British, French, or Italian rule. What used to be Anglo-Egyptian Sudan refused to be ruled by Egypt when the joint Anglo-Egyptian rule terminated. The African countries are not only against rule from outside Africa, but also from within Africa itself. Each African country likes to be independent of another African country, just as Britain likes to be independent of France, and France of Britain.

Whatever merits a foreign rule may have, the fact remains that the essence of foreign rule is the imposition of the will of foreigners on the natives of the country. It is the deprivation of the freedom of other people. The African is aware of this. The bitter lessons of history have thoroughly impressed him with the humiliating experience of living under foreign rule.

But here again let us be clear. Suppose Africa was taken over by Russian communists, what distinct advantage would she have, if any? Most educated Africans with whom we have discussed this matter seem to be unanimous that the only difference there would be is 'the exchange of reins'. The African would still be foreign-ruled. He has been a puppet in the hands of European imperialists, and he would remain one in the hands of Russian communists. The question is not whether Africans prefer European imperialism to Russian communism, or vice versa. They prefer neither. They prefer to rule themselves to being ruled by foreigners. There is not a single African from any one of these independent sovereign African states we have talked to who does not subscribe fully to this strong sentiment we have sensed again and again: 'We want to be ourselves. If we succeed we want the credit to come to us, not to go to Russia or to Europe. If we fail we want to benefit from our mistakes.'

A brief account of the situation in European-ruled Africa will further serve to show why we believe that African history, as a whole, has conditioned the African against foreign rule, and why we think that this fact is a bulwark against the spread of communism to various African countries. The Africans, as a people, have suffered physically and spiritually under foreign rule, and their history is the living testimony of this.

Let us begin with British Central Africa. In 1888 Cecil John Rhodes concluded an agreement with King Lobengula and acquired the exclusive metal and mineral rights in what is now Southern Rhodesia. In 1893 Rhodes and his companions deliberately provoked the Matabele into a war which left Rhodes in sole possession of the entire country. The British South Africa Company seized and stole the cattle of the Matabele, and up to this day the Matabele still speak of their cattle which were stolen by the 'white dogs'. In 1896 the Matabele and the Mashona rose in a rebellion against British rule, but they were successfully defeated. In 1923 the country now called Southern Rhodesia ceased to be administered by the British South Africa Company and was annexed to the British Crown. From 1893 until this day (1957) the African people have been subjected to severe and humiliating discriminatory laws, although improvements have been made here and there over the years.

Northern Rhodesia was occupied by the British at the same time as Southern Rhodesia, but never by force of arms. Her chiefs made treaties with Queen Victoria. Hence, while the native people of Northern Rhodesia freely asked for British protection, they unwittingly asked for British domination as well. Protection without domination is almost impossible. Now that the Northern Rhodesia African National Congress has awakened to the idea of freedom and full independence, the British government will not remove the protection which Queen Victoria promised their chiefs. Mr. Harry Nkumbula, its president, and other members of the Congress have suffered imprisonment because they agitated for African freedom and self-determination. The Northern Rhodesia African Mineworkers' Trade Union, founded in 1949, also labours under great handicaps deliberately thrown in its way by the government. The industrial colour bar is a European device to render the union ineffective. In brief, the African in Northern Rhodesia, like his counterpart in Southern Rhodesia, is a humiliated citizen in the land of his birth.

When the referendum of the Federation of Rhodesia and Nyasaland came, practically all Nyasalanders were against it. Chief Philip Gomani and about eighty other chiefs were also dead against it. But the government did not respect the will of the native people. A state of emergency was declared and many chiefs were placed under arrest, and, that being done, the Federation was imposed on Nyasaland. Up to this day the Nyasalanders have not been reconciled to Federation. They had hoped that, under the auspices of the Nyasaland African National Congress, led by President J. S. Sangala, July 1957 was going to see them a free independent country, but events have smashed their hopes to pieces.

In these three countries we have dealt with we see how the British will has been imposed upon the people, not only by cunning diplomacy, but by military power and police action. We see how little the wishes of the African people count when they collide with those of the British. African chiefs are merely British puppets. But any foreign power would do as the British are doing.

British East Africa shows the same trends. Tanganyika was a German territory from the 1880's to World War I. In 1898 Chief Quawa committed suicide to avoid capture by the Germans who were trying to subdue all the native tribes. In 1903-5 the Maji-Maji rebellion against the Germans took place. The Angoni tribe of southern Tanganyika were the chief instigators. They resented foreign domination. But the Germans, with their usual thorough expert killing, ruthlessly put down the rebellion which cost the lives of 120,000 Africans. In 1914-18 the British conquered Tanganyika, and thus put an end to the German protectorate. Now Tanganyika is a United Nations Trust Territory administered by the British. In 1955 the report on the Trust Territory spoke of the possibility of Tanganyika having her independence in this generation. This greatly angered the British who maintained that Tanganyika is not ready for independence.

Uganda is the next British East African country we want to consider briefly. The British took Buganda in 1893, and seven years later the whole of Uganda fell under British sway, not by force of arms, but by the Uganda Agreement of 1900. Uganda has been comparatively peaceful, but the Uganda African National Congress, which is so much opposed to the British 'divide and rule' method, is also bitterly opposed to European immigration lest Uganda become another Kenya or Southern Rhodesia (with strong white settlements and repressive native policy). The Nationalists want Uganda to remain a black man's country, and they want the same sovereign independence as the Sudan (formerly, Anglo-Egyptian Sudan) now enjoys.

The crisis of the Kabaka of Uganda serves as a good illustration of how the Africans in general view foreign rule. When Oliver Lyttelton, then Colonial Secretary in London, made a passing remark that Uganda, Kenya, and Tanganyika might federate, the suspicions of the Kabaka of Buganda were aroused that the British government intended forcing federation against the wishes of the people as it had done in the case of Nyasaland. The Kabaka wanted, therefore, to separate Buganda from Uganda, that is, from the Colonial Office, so that what would befall the rest of Uganda in the way of federation with Kenya and Tanganyika might not affect her. When the Governor, Sir Andrew Cohen, tried to bring about reform measures in the whole of Uganda, which includes Buganda, the Kabaka construed these measures as a surreptitious effort to impose federation, and in June 1953 he openly opposed them. The Governor viewed this as an act of insubordination, and in November of the same year the Kabaka was flown to London by way of deposition, thus demonstrating once for all that a British governor had a higher status than an African king, and that an African king under British protection was but a puppet of a British governor. In 1955, however, the Kabaka was returned and restored to his former position, but the lesson went home that protected independence was but a sham. Only self-rule can ensure the dignity of a people.

It would be monotonous to go into a brief history of Kenya. It flows more or less in the same direction as other British countries. And so we now come to that of the Belgian Congo. Here again our aim is to show that the African knows the hardships of being under foreign rule.

After the Berlin Conference of 1884-5 the Congo basin fell to the personal ownership of King Leopold I of Belgium, who ruled it from 1885 to 1908. In 1908 the Belgian Congo was transferred to the Belgian government. The well-known 'Congo atrocities' need not delay us here, but it is worth noting that during King Leopold's reign, that is from 1885 to 1908, between 5,000,000 and 8,000,000 Africans were killed by European traders and administrators who sought ivory and rubber. Those who failed to bring the required quota of rubber were repulsively mutilated. Sometimes their hands or feet were cut off, and this method of mutilation was exclusively European, not African. Perhaps the following quotations will paint the picture much better than we can:

'S.S. Van Kerkhoven is coming down the Nile and will demand 1,500 porters. Unlucky niggers! I can hardly bear to think of them. I am asking myself how on earth I shall be able to hunt up so large a number. . . . Marshes, hunger, exhaustion. How much blood will be shed because of this transport! Three times, already, I have had to make war upon the chiefs who could not help me to get the men I needed. The fellows would rather die in their own forests than as members of a transport train. If a chief refuses, that means war, with modern fire-arms on one side against spears and javelins on the other!

'The inhabitants have disappeared. Their homes have been burned; huge heaps of ashes amid neglected palm-hedges and devastated abandoned fields. Inhuman floggings, murders, plunderings and carryings-off.'[1]

All these things were done by the so-called civilized people against the so-called savage Africans! Things, however, have changed since the Leopold regime was replaced by the Belgian

[1] Ludwig Bauer: *Leopold the Unloved* (Cassell), quoted by T. W. Wallbank: *Contemporary Africa*, p. 111.

government. But the memory of these European brutalities is still very vivid to many Africans, and it is passed from generation to generation.

We may now ask ourselves this question: What is the real significance of the facts we have recounted? In all European-ruled Africa, the black man has suffered untold humiliation. (There is a sense in which a people suffer under self-rule, but there is also a sense in which a people suffer under alien rule. The difference being that under self-rule a people suffer with dignity, but under alien rule, with imposed humiliation.) His life, particularly during the early days of European occupation of Africa, has been, in the eyes of the Europeans, a little better than that of wild animals. From Cape to Cairo and from the African horn in the East to the African bulge in the West, the African has had a collective experience of being ruled by a foreign power, and it is this collective experience that promises to be one of the formidable factors against communist penetration in Africa. To the African —educated or uneducated—the present European powers are no different from Russia. They are all foreign powers. Russians are just as white as the French, Belgians, British, or any other European nationalities. They are just as ambitious. It is true that communists promise to give subject peoples freedom and independence, but it is equally true that communism aims at world domination, and this also means African subjugation. The thinking African is aware of this. To support Russia is to support his own subjection, and the same thing is true when he supports the present European rule.

History has taught the African many things. The French occupied North, West, and Equatorial Africa in the name of protection, but that turned out to be humiliating domination. The British occupied Central, East, and West Africa, in the name of protection, but that turned out to be humiliating domination. The Portuguese occupied Mozambique and Angola in the name of protection, but that also turned out to be humiliating domination. The Belgians occupied what is now the Belgian Congo, and that also turned out to be humiliating domination. And it does not require any stretch of imagination to see that if Russia occupied any part of Africa, that also would be humiliating domination. As the uneducated Africans put it, 'Foreign rule is the same'. What they mean is that it is humiliating to be ruled by foreigners. Foreign rule, from the point of view of the subject peoples, has no meaning outside humiliation, and from the vantage point of the foreign ruler it has no meaning outside political ascendancy.

It seems to us, therefore, that if the present colonial powers had never occupied Africa, the present communism would easily make inroads into the very heart of Africa, since the African would not have had the experience of being under foreign rule. The African would never have developed that inner frame of reference by which to judge the many attractive promises of the communists. He would easily fall a victim of communism just as he did in the case of European imperialism. Happily, European imperialism forestalled communism in the sense that while it antagonized the African against itself, it also set the African against communism.

Thus it seems as if Providence saw through the long corridors of time and space the distant forward march of communism and hastened, in the nineteenth century, to send colonial powers to Africa to inoculate all the peoples of Africa with such anti-communisms as have now rendered the African immune against the communist virus that is threatening freedom with extinction. We believe it would be true to say that enough resistance against communism has been built up in the African people as a whole, whether or not they are conscious of it. But this is not by any means to suggest that all African people are proof against communism. We are here merely accounting for the factors that explain why the educated Africans, in whose hands now rests African political leadership, are so much opposed to communism. We believe it is only an educated African imbecile who will trade the present European imperialism for Russian communism. He may as well sit down and suck his thumb under the present European imperialism and be quiet.

But, as we have already indicated, the African may take to communism as a desperate measure. He might use communism willingly as an instrument (though a very dangerous one) to get his full independence. But this is only a supposition. So far there are no cases we know of where a group of African people have organized themselves into a communist party. The Mau Mau movement was popularly said to be communist-inspired. This statement was made partly because of suspicious ignorance, and partly as a sympathy-fishing device on the part of the white people. The whole movement was Kikuyu-inspired. The following extract supports this:

'There is no evidence that communism or communists' agents have had any direct or indirect part in the organization or direction of the Mau Mau itself, or its activities. Jomo Kenyatta, its leader, visited Moscow some time before 1947. But there is no evidence of communist technique in the organization and activities of the movement, which are in an African idiom. . . .'[1]

It is interesting to notice that even the Mau Mau had nothing to do with communism. In Ghana the government has banned the Communist Party, though in Britain, France, and India the Communist Party enjoys legal recognition. As one Ghana student put it, 'The Communist Party represents foreign rule that aims at world subjection. And we will have none of it.'

Africa as a whole seems well fortified against communism since both the European powers and the African people have been conditioned against it. Africa as a whole has been predominantly Westernized economically, politically, socially, ideologically, and educationally. Practically all highly educated Africans have been Western-educated. The Russianization of Africa is a possibility immediate or remote, but not a fact, whereas the Westernization of Africa is an accomplished fact that has historical roots. Even at present thousands of African students being educated overseas are in British, West European, and American colleges. Millions of Africans speak English, French, Portuguese, and Spanish, but we have not met one who speaks Russian. What we are trying to say here is that there is already a common ground between the West and Africa, and this common ground is based on practical interests, and this is why we believe

[1] Wallbank, op. cit., p. 154.

that if the African people ceased to be treated like strangers in the land of their birth, a genuine understanding between black and white would develop and this in turn would strengthen the anti-communist forces.

So far as we have examined our topic, we find no relation between African nationalism and Russian communism. African nationalism springs from inside Africa, and not from Moscow. If the African can continue to hate communism with all his heart, and soul, and might, just as he does European imperialism, so much to the good, because to prefer one brand of imperialism to another is the very height of folly and a fatal miscalculation. Africa can derive no more and no less benefit from communism than from European imperialism. Her real welfare does not lie in preferring either one or the other, but in rejecting both, since under one or the other she will continue to occupy a secondary position and suffer the indignities that go with such a position.

CHAPTER TWELVE

The Cracking Myth

When thinking of a suitable title for the present chapter, several titles suggested themselves. The first one was 'The Exploding Myth', but this did not express accurately the idea we had in mind since 'explosion' is sudden and noisy but soon expends itself. It also lacks that continuous process which can be measured in years. It comes and goes. Then we thought of another possible title, 'The Siege of the Citadel'. But this also did not satisfy us because it suggested the idea of a highly organized army trying to capture some booty. It suggested deliberate planning, conscious manoeuvres and purposeful encroachment; but, so far, what we wish to describe here has no conscious design. Finally we settled on our present title, and this proved satisfactory since it excludes any conscious element, and since it shows a subtle but effective process, by almost imperceptible degrees, covering many decades. Like the plant whose various stages of growth we cannot see with our naked eyes, although we can see the total growth, so is the cracking process. First, there is a very tiny crack to a point of invisibility, and our attention is not drawn to it. Then there is the small visible crack, but too small to attract serious attention. Then there comes that type which manages to stir up some concern, followed by one which causes real concern. Finally there is the complete act of cracking which causes the downfall of the structure.

Africa has been inhabited by a myth, and that myth is now cracking. In some areas it has reached the last point of falling asunder; in others it is showing only very serious cracks without falling apart; and in yet other areas it suffers only insignificant cracks.

The first time he ever came into contact with the white man, the African was simply overwhelmed, overawed, puzzled, perplexed, mystified, and dazzled. The white man's 'houses that move on the water', his 'bird that is not like other birds', 'his monster that spits fire and smoke and swallows people and spits them out alive', his ability to 'kill' a man and again raise him from the dead (anaesthesia), his big massive and impressive house that had many other houses in it (the house that has houses, the Matabele used to say), and many new things introduced by the white man just amazed the African. Motor-cars, motor cycles, bicycles, gramophones, telegraphy, the telephone, glittering Western clothes, new ways of ploughing and planting, added to the African's sense of curiosity and novelty. Never before had the African seen such things. They were beyond his comprehension; they were outside the realm of his experience. He saw. He wondered. He mused. He trembled at the sight of the white man whose prestige soared sky-high and left the African bowing before this new white god who had come from the waters of the ocean. Here then the African came into contact with two-legged gods who chose to dwell among people instead of in the distant mountains. For the first time he came in contact with gods who had wives and children, and who kept dogs and cats.

These new white gods were conscious of the magic spell they had cast over the Africans, and they did everything to maintain it. They demonstrated their control of the lightning by firing their guns regularly, and this, to the ears of the Africans, sounded like thunder in the sky. There was hardly anything that the white man did which had no god-like aspects to it. The African, who never argues with his gods lest their wrath visit him, adopted the same attitude to the white man because he was, to him, a god. Woe unto him who argues with the new gods from over the seas! And so the Africans submitted themselves to the rule of the white man without question. The white man became master in the house that was not his. He ordered the African right and left and the African was only too ready to please his white god. And the white man saw that it was good, and he smiled with deep satisfaction and said 'Africa, the White Man's Paradise'. Any other race of human beings could have done the same thing under similar circumstances.

At this juncture we are reminded of the great Captain Cook who played the role of a god when he and his crew landed on one of the Hawaiian islands, where the natives, having never seen anyone like him and his crew before, and having never seen or heard a gun before, quickly fell on their faces and worshipped him for they thought he was a god who had come from the sky. His crew they took for lesser gods. And so they gave him the full liberty of their temple where they enthroned him as their god. They were delighted that they, of all the peoples of the earth, had been very lucky in that the gods had chosen to visit them. Here was the chosen tribe of the Hawaiians. But as time went on some of the more intelligent among the natives began to doubt the 'godness' of the new god for he had all the externals of any one among them. Sooner or later the natives were divided into two schools of thought—those who believed that Captain Cook was a genuine god, and those who took him for only a fake god. To argue for or against without practical demonstration, affirming or disproving, neither side was convinced until one day, one among them who was apparently endowed with intelligence above the ordinary range, picked up a stone, and with a good aim, and with all his might, hurled it against god Captain Cook. The brave Captain Cook felt the full impact of the stone and winced with pain, whereupon the untutored Hawaiian scientist triumphantly exclaimed, 'He feels pain. Therefore he is not a god.' Great was the fury of the natives who had come to worship their god. They soon realized that he was only a fake god, and like hungry and angry hounds they fell upon their god, and thus died another pretender to the throne of the gods.

Right from the beginning relations between the Africans and the white people were strictly controlled and regulated. The white man made laws forbidding intermarriage and cohabitation between black and white so that this white magic spell might continue to work to the maximum benefit of the white man. A death penalty was attached to violation of this law, but this was only applicable to the African male. To the African the law appeared quite unnecessary. 'How can a man cohabit with a goddess?' they asked innocently. 'How can a woman cohabit with a god?' they still wondered. To the African the word 'man' meant an African male, and the word 'woman' an African female.

The white male and his female, both inhabited a higher world —that of gods and goddesses. The Matabele, the brave and warlike tribe that broke away from the Zulu nation, called the white people *Omlimu abadla amabele*—the gods that eat corn. The gods the Matabele had known never ate any food. Although the Matabele made this distinction, nevertheless the only difference they saw between the gods they had known and these white gods was that the latter lived on actual food. In life these 'gods who eat corn' were feared above the gods the Matabele had known, the reason being that the white gods were near and visible and acted visibly whereas the usual gods were distant and invisible. The early relations between black and white in many parts of Africa were those of god and creature whose life was at the mercy of the god.

The African stood and folded his hands, and gazed, and waited for the white gods to tell him what to do next. He feared to move on his own lest he court for himself their vengeful wrath. Deep mines were opened throughout the country. The dynamite that exploded the huge rocks still confirmed the African's belief that the white man was a god. The African soon noticed that the white man 'has untold material wealth' and had the ability of creating even more. He soon associated all power, wealth, skills, cleverness, wisdom, and knowledge with the white man. While by nature the African does not like to stay too close to the quarters of the gods whose actions were so unpredictable, and whose fury was like a consuming fire, yet he was compelled to stay near these white gods who demanded his labour. The African soon noticed that all his people had been turned into a nation of servants of the white man, and in all fairness, many of these thoroughly enjoyed themselves by dwelling in the house of the Lord for ever. And who would not rejoice to work for the gods to escape destruction?

But soon the African, while admitting to himself that there was a world of difference between himself and the white man, vaguely sensed much that was in common between him and the white man. The Matabele were not altogether wrong when they referred to the white people as 'gods who eat corn'. According

to the Matabele philosophy anything that eats corn dies. The
fact of eating corn is the fact of mortality on the part of the eater
since corn itself today is, and tomorrow is no more. In short,
unconsciously, the Matabele had sensed that beyond the white
man was *uNkulunkulu*—the Great, Great one—*uSimakade*—the
one who has always stood over and against us—of whom they
sang thus:

> *INkosi yasidabula ngamandla*
> *Ilensiba ezimnyama*
> *Ezahlatshelelwa ngameva.*
> (The Lord created us with his strength
> He has black wings that are adorned with thorns.)

But how could they reconcile this theological belief with these
new wonders of the white man? The instinct of self-preservation
that inclined towards treating the white man like a god triumphed
temporarily over very strong theological doubts.

There was a time, since the European occupation of Africa,
when the white skin seemed to be all that mattered, when it was
mistaken for power and success in the world. There was a time
in Africa when the African people thought that perhaps if they
had a European name that would guarantee to them success in
life. African Christian converts took on Western names. How
could they possibly be genuine Christians without some Bible
name? How could they possibly get along with the white man if
all their names were African? African pastors and evangelists
demanded that every African convert have a Bible name. The
essence of genuine Christianity was in the Bible name and not
so much in the heart of the individual. Some Africans European-
ized their names. And so African 'Jabulani Tendele Sibanda'
became 'John Philip Brown'. In some areas the process of taking
on European names is still in vogue, though the motive has
changed.

The psychology of all this was to identify themselves with the
conqueror—to enlist the sympathy of the gods. To have no
European name became a thing to be ashamed of, a kind of social
stigma, a symbol of backwardness. Indeed there was magic in the

European name. It seemed to open up to the African all sorts of fantastic worlds. Anything that had anything to do with the white man had something bordering on magic. Black heroes were pushed into the background so that for some time every hero was white, and every white man was a hero. The black man became the villain in the theatre of life. So for a time the white man held the stage while his spellbound African spectators just gazed and gazed and wondered about this new creature upon whom God seemed to have showered all the blessings of life. For a time the white man became the North Pole and his African admirers, so highly charged with the magnetic power, were easily attracted to him, and this greatly enhanced the myth.

I still can remember as if it were yesterday, although it is now twenty years ago, when African students in Southern Rhodesia used to resent being taught by an African teacher. They preferred, regardless of everything else, a white teacher to a black teacher. To them the white skin had come to mean good teaching, and the black skin bad teaching. I remember a personal incident. Some of my pupils actually wept that they had been given a black teacher instead of a white one. They had never seen me teach before. They were new-comers, and yet they had already prejudged that I was not a good teacher. Why? Because I was black and there the matter ended. The white teacher they had also prejudged although they had never known him before as a teacher. What was their standard of measure? The colour of his skin. The white skin had real magic even for African students. But now all this has changed. The African students now lump together a stupid black teacher with a stupid white teacher, and a clever black teacher with a clever white teacher. The African student has progressed to a point when he sees no relation between a teacher's ability and the colour of his skin. He now judges the teacher not by the colour of his skin but by his teaching ability. The white teachers no longer enjoy prestige above African teachers on the ground of the colour of their skin. Whatever prestige they now enjoy is based on merit alone. The African teacher no longer suffers on the ground of the colour of his skin. He now enjoys considerable prestige, meritoriously earned, like his white colleague. The centre of gravity has shifted from colour to merit.

Time is a great doctor. It heals up many things. It clarifies many things. It reveals many things. It does all kinds of things. Winter cannot boast that it holds sway over the entire universe all the time, for sooner or later summer sets in to discredit the claim. Nor can summer boast on the same ground. The white man could play the part of a god only within a limited duration of time, not indefinitely. He could remain a myth, a mystery, only subject to human limitations. The myth was bound to show cracks here and there as Time rolled on to Eternity. And soon the African discovered that the white man, after all, was God-created. He had not created himself. There were various factors that brought the African's attention to this realization.

We shall begin on the domestic level. The African observed rather curiously that his own domestic life closely resembled that of the white man. When the African saw that the white female became pregnant like his own wife, that sometimes both the white male and female had a fight, that sometimes white males fought over a white female, that sometimes an angry-with-wife white male refused to eat when he was offered food by his wife, that both the white male and white female wrinkled and stooped with age, that white people also died, he was reminded of the experiences he had had in his domestic life, and gradually he began to see through the myth, darkly but not face to face, to borrow the Apostle Paul's language.

But this revelation did not stop only at the white man's domestic side of life. It extended to the African's domestic side of life as well. The white male, for some reason or other, became intensely interested in African women. When an African found a white male in the arms of an African female he was horrified to the core of his being, for woe unto the eyes that saw the gods take such liberties. The African who had seen this god-human spectacle made sure that such an experience remained a sealed book. He feared to arouse the anger of the gods who would not only punish his iniquities but would visit these on the members of his community. As more and more of these white males were found relaxing in the very congenial society of African ladies, the news began to be proclaimed from hilltop to hilltop in sheer amusement. The African males sarcastically warned, 'Take care of our women. The gods have partaken of the forbidden fruit of Africa, and may forget their own women.' Next, the African began to resent the white man's liberties with the African female while many an African male was sent to the gallows for cohabiting with white females, some of whom were as fond of an African male as some African women were of white males. And thus on the domestic level the white man and his female were stripped of their 'god aspects' and stood naked, before the African, like ordinary human beings. 'They were deceiving us', said the African. 'We are the same.'

The narrow-minded African blamed the white male for interfering with his women, but the broad-minded rejoiced, partly because this gave a lie to the altogether common statement that whites and blacks were basically different, and partly because they were pleased to see that despite the fact that the white man boasted of two thousand years of civilization and culture behind him, he succumbed to the African madonna. White governors, M.P.s, medical doctors, lawyers, top business men, postmasters, ministers of religion, and other top executives, not to speak of the lower classes, all capitulated to the irresistible charms of the African madonna. This is not to deny the fact that African males also fell down at the feet of white madonnas and forgot all about their black madonnas. This should not surprise us because both the African male and the white male have the same thing in common, and that is the 'male principle'. Both the African madonna and the white madonna have also the same thing in common, and that is the 'female principle'. The male principle, regardless of race or colour, finds its practical expression in the female principle regardless of colour or race. Conversely the female principle seeks satisfaction in the male principle also regardless of colour or race.

There was a time in Africa when the white male's actions towards African women were said to arise from the fact that there were very few white females in Africa, but although there are now almost as many white women as white men, the white male still roams the African female world. The male principle will continue to seek out the female principle regardless of this or that colour or race or nationality. In short, what we are trying to say here is that the white myth which had so overwhelmed the African could not remain the same after the white male had slept with an African female, and after the African male had slept with a white female. The myth was unveiled in many places, and is still being unveiled. Some white racialists, to restore this myth to its former dignity, try to tighten up on race relations between males and females; but alas, once the forbidden fruit has been tasted withdrawal is impossible. As long as people still have the appetite they will continue to eat the forbidden fruit.

There was a time when all teachers, ministers of religion, prime ministers, lawyers, judges, magistrates, medical doctors, journalists, men of letters, clerks, policemen, train, crane and tractor drivers, postmasters, retail and wholesale merchants, and the like, were exclusively white. It was during this time that the black man used to condemn God for creating him black—for blackness had become for him synonymous with inability, foolishness, and backwardness. It was at this time that the African was beginning, after accepting that the white man was not a god, but a human being, to question whether or not the clay that went to make his mortal body was the same as that which went to make the body of the white man. When Dr. Aggrey of the Gold Coast (now Ghana) said, 'A man who is not proud of his colour is not fit to live', he was trying to correct this self-deprecating, apologetic attitude of many an African. As long as all important positions remained exclusively white, the myth held together and cast its magic spell over the African. But when an army of black teachers, ministers of religion, prime ministers, lawyers, judges, magistrates, medical doctors, journalists, men of letters, clerks, policemen, train, crane and tractor drivers, postmasters, retail and wholesale merchants, and the like, made their appearance on the African scene, the white myth began to show more cracks. The African saw more clearly than ever before that what mattered was not whether or not one was white or black, but whether or not one had the necessary skills, the necessary training. The magic was no longer in the colour of the skin but rather in the acquisition of the highest skills. It still thrills the African to perform as well as the white man. Everywhere African efficiency is helping the white myth to crack more and more, and the thinking white man is conscious of this, and he is accordingly changing his psychological approach to the African.

About fifteen years ago, a white friend of mine in Southern Rhodesia used to say to me, 'Sithole, it pays for a black man to get highly educated, but it does not pay the same dividends for a white man'. My friend was quite confident that the white skin, at least in Southern Rhodesia, was enough to ensure the white man's success. But events in Southern Rhodesia have belied him since now African M.P.s, lawyers, solicitors, and men of letters have appeared on the Rhodesian scene. Events are cracking the white myth. Qualifications and merit bid fair to push into the background the colour of a man's skin, and to occupy the foreground.

World Wars I and II also helped the cracks of the white myth to widen. Thousands of African soldiers went abroad on active service. The English street-girls of London, the French street-girls of Paris, and the Italian street-girls of Naples did not help the preservation of the white myth. Drinking and woman-raping white soldiers still added their contribution towards the annihilation of this myth. The African soldiers were ordered by the white commanders to kill white enemy soldiers. The African soldiers from Southern and Northern Rhodesia, Nyasaland, Tanganyika, Kenya, North Africa, French West Africa, French Equatorial Africa, the Gold Coast, and Nigeria, found themselves at the front line of war with one purpose in view: to kill every white enemy soldier they could get hold of. Many German and Italian soldiers fell victims to shots fired by African soldiers.

The African soldiers saw white soldiers wounded, dying, and dead. The bullet had the same effect on black and white alike. This had a very powerful psychological impact on the African. He saw what he used to call his betters suffer defeat, though not conquest, at the hands of the Germans and Japanese, and once more he was impressed by the fact that it was not being white or black that mattered but the necessary training in these things. The veil between him and the white man thinned to a point of transparency, and at other points it disappeared altogether. After suffering side by side with his white fellow-soldiers the African never again regarded them in the same light. After spending four years hunting white enemy soldiers the African never regarded them again as gods.

But now we ask ourselves this question: What has this to do with the problem of the rise of African nationalism? The emergent African nationalism, in many ways, represents the degree to which the white man's magic spell, which at the beginning of the nineteenth century had been cast on the African, is wearing off. As long as this myth was thick and impenetrable, the African adjusted himself as well as he could to what he thought were gods, though gods that ate corn. As long as the white man was able to hold up his pretensions to the African as real, the African was scared, and never challenged the white man as his national ruler. Alas, the externals have had their day, and reality has taken its place; but few white people in Africa realize this extremely important change. Most of them still have the picture of the African who worships the white man as a god, and they refuse to face the fact that Time and Eternity are beckoning to them to come down from their ivory towers and dwell among their fellow-creatures for their own sake and for that of their fellow-creatures.

There are certain basic facts that these white people, who would like to be regarded by Africans as myth, forget. The generation of Africans who first came into contact with the white man and his wonders were overwhelmed by the novelty of the white man and the new things he had brought to Africa. It was natural therefore to accord the white man a special place in Africa. But a good part of the present African generation, born in modern hospitals, raised in modern towns and cities, educated in modern schools, travelling by land, air, and sea, using the most up-to-date means of conveyance, trained in modern arts and skills, employed in modern factories, mines, and other occupations, rubbing shoulders daily with white people in towns, cities, schools, and on the battlefield, take the white man as a matter of course, just as they take another African in the same way. They know no other environment. The white man can no longer cast his spell over them by the simple trick of showing them the train or an automobile, or reading to them a story book, or cracking his gun, because many an African now knows how to do these things. It pains the white man to realize that the African now regards him as an ordinary human being. To him the new African generation is all degenerate. It has no proper respect for the white man, not so much because he is human but because he is white. Here then is the dilemma of the white man. He fails to draw a distinction between what was and what is, let alone what will be in a matter of a few decades. He fails to grasp what has happened since his coming to Africa.

This aspect raises the question: How much African is the present-day African? There is a world of difference between the African prior to the coming of the white man and the African after Africa was occupied by European powers. There is therefore a sense in which an African is African, and a sense in which he is not African, just as there is a sense in which an American who has spent two-thirds of his life in Africa is and is not American, and is and is not African. While the Westerners may be consciously Westernizing Africa, Africa is also unconsciously Africanizing them. The interaction between the West and Africa is producing a new brand of the African. That is, it is pushing the white-man-worshipping African into the background, and bringing into the foreground the African who does not worship the white man. The proud and arrogant African may think he is 100 per cent African because both his mother and father are African, just as a proud and arrogant white man born in Africa may also think he is 100 per cent European. The truth is that there is no such thing in a multiracial society as 100 per cent this or that race.

Take an African who has been to school. He may think he is 100 per cent African. Externally and physically this may be true. But an examination of the content of his consciousness, even on a superficial level, will disclose that his mathematical thought, his legal training, his theological views, his commercial and industrial understanding, his economic theories, the themes of his conversation, his present aspirations and hopes, to quote only a few, are radically different from those of an African who lived before the advent of European powers. We are not suggesting here that there is a clean break between the present-day African and his forefathers. We recognize fully a sense of historical continuity, and yet, at the same time, we recognize self-evident economic, political, and social discontinuity between the African and his ancestors. The present-day African has new eyes, as it were. He sees new things that he never saw before. He has new ears. He hears new things that he never heard before. He has a new sensibility. He feels things that he never felt before. He does not see what his forefathers saw. He does not hear what his forefathers heard. He does not feel what his forefathers felt. He does not see the white myth his forefathers saw, for the simple reason that he has ceased in many ways to be the African his forefathers used to be. He is not like his forefathers. Why not? His forefathers lived during the period when the pace was set by the wagon; but he lives during the period when electricity sets the pace.

But in what way is the present African really different from his forefathers? The answer is simple. His forefathers were vaguely conscious of the country in which they lived. They were not conscious of the rest of Africa—certainly not of the countries outside Africa. This was specially true of those who lived inland, but not so true of those who lived along the coast. They spent most of their time looking after their livestock, hunting and trapping game. Perhaps to describe their lot negatively may be helpful here. Their eyes never saw the large cities and towns whose buildings now soar to the sky. They never rode bicycles, motor-cars, trains, and they never flew. They never went to school; that is, they never learned how to read and write. They never built themselves modern houses. In short, their period was marked by the widespread absence of modern facilities and conveniences, and hence, from their point of view, the white man was just a myth. This gives us a new angle of vision so that we may rightly say that a myth depends for its existence upon our ignorance. As soon as this ignorance is removed, the myth also is removed.

The modern African, on the other hand, lives in an environment in many instances totally different from that in which his forefathers lived. He is not only conscious of the country in which he lives, but also of Africa as a whole, and of the whole world. International forces play on his conscious being in a way his forefathers never experienced. Unlike his forefathers' environment that hummed with bees, and that was livened with singing birds, disturbed by wild animals, and moved at nature's pace, the modern African now lives in an environment where the mechanical bird has superseded the bird, where automobiles, trains, and tractors have pushed the ox, the donkey, and the horse into the background. He lives in an atmosphere in which his forefathers' myth lived. If the African forefathers should come back to life and behold their own descendants on the modern scene, it is not far-fetched to say they would mistake their own children for the gods.

In many ways it is correct to talk of the latter half of the twentieth century as the de-mythification of the white man in Africa. If it were in his power, the average white man would like to push the African back into the days of the white myth, but this is now impossible. Time has given birth to a new African who is more self-asserting, more enterprising, more aggressive, and more self-reliant than his forebears. It is impossible to push this new African back into Time's womb just as the baby once expelled from its mother's womb cannot begin a successful 'back-to-the-womb' movement. This can only be a wasted effort. The baby has to cope as well as it can with the out-of-womb conditions. Even the African himself is trying to cope as well as he can with the new times into which he has been born. Anyone who advises him to behave as his forefathers behaved towards white people may as well advise him to return into his mother's womb. Most thinking white people accept this important change, and meet the situation as it is without wasting time and effort in wishful thinking. But the attitude of the average white man is like that of dethroned gods. Their paradise is passing away with the emergence of this new African, and they will struggle hard to retain it.

The now politically conscious African reminds us of Shakespeare's Caliban who mistook the new-comers to the island for gods, and immediately pledged his loyalty to them. In his own words we can see the psychological impact Stephano and his friends had made on Caliban during their first encounter with him:

> *Caliban* [aside]: These be fine things an if they be not sprites. That's a brave god and bears celestial liquor: I will kneel to him.
>
> . . .
>
> *Caliban*: I'll swear upon that bottle, to be thy true subject; for the liquor is not earthly.
>
> . . .
>
> *Caliban*: I'll show thee every fertile inch o' the island; and I will kiss thy foot: I prithee, be my god.[1]

Caliban had been thoroughly impressed that Stephano, the drunken butler, was a god from heaven. But after Time had taken its course to reveal the true nature of his new god, Caliban makes his confession:

> . . . and I'll be wise hereafter,
> And seek for grace. What a thrice-double ass
> Was I, to take this drunkard for a god,
> And worship this dull fool![2]

There was a time in the history of European occupation of Africa when the African people became so dependent on the European people that they vied with one another for the white man's favour. The African teachers, for instance, if they had a genuine grievance against the Native Education Department, were afraid to face the Department, and employed the services of one of their sympathetic missionaries or other white men who had their interest at heart to speak for them. The same thing—

[1] *The Tempest*, II, ii.
[2] Op. cit., v, i.

that is, employing white people to fight for them—was true of African politicians, farmers, merchants, and different African associations. They chose a white spokesman to face the white government for them. But now the whole pattern has changed. The African teachers have organized themselves into various African teachers' associations, the African politicians into the national congress, the farmers into African farmers' associations, the business men into African business men's associations, and so on. It is the African office-bearers themselves who now fight directly for better conditions for their people. They are no longer afraid to come out into the open and say what they feel and think. A big psychological mountain-top experience has been reached. More and more the African's childlike spirit of dependence is decreasing, and he is rapidly showing a spirit of independence.

One might compare the early relation between black and white to that between child and parent. So long as the child is dependent upon the parents, they easily secure his loyalty and obedience, and so long as the child remains child, there is always something mythical about parents, from the viewpoint of the child. My wife, when she was 10, and not my wife then, used to think her mother was a wonderful woman because she had brought into the world her four brothers and two sisters, and when her mother told her that one day she would also bring into the world babies, she used to say, 'No. Impossible. I am not like you.' Her mother was always a mystery to her. But since then my wife has brought five children into the world, and when her mother reminded her of what she used to say, she would only smile, as if to say, 'I should have known better'. As long as she was ignorant of the facts of childbirth, the myth about her mother held together, and presented an impenetrable wall to her, but as soon as she knew the facts of childbirth, the mystery fell asunder and shattered altogether, never to be reconstructed.

As soon as the African knew how to read and write, how to drive and repair an automobile, how to build a modern house and install modern plumbing, how to operate properly on a human body, how to run a business properly, how to do countless other things that his white god did, why, the myth fell asunder, never to come together again. As long as the African did not know these things, the myth remained intact, impressive and impenetrable. To cry for the return of the myth is like crying for the return of general ignorance in a world of general enlightenment. The tide of human affairs today does not permit the comfortable existence of myths, be they black or white or yellow or brown. Modern hospitals and science and technology are exploding the mythical existence of the African witchdoctor, and by the same token that of the white man. Only those who are willing to swim with the tide, rather than against it, have any hope of finding their balance in multiracial Africa.

However, we must not be understood to imply that all Africans have emerged from their primitive stage. As a matter of fact the majority have not. But in all revolutions it is the minority that counts. In any country a vocal minority has brought about undreamt-of changes. The educated African minority is a force that cannot be ignored without disastrous results. While the majority of Africans may still acknowledge the white myth here and there, and doubt it here and there, the educated African has not the time for it. It simply does not exist, and what counts is what the educated African thinks and does, since he is the one who is now the spokesman of his people.

But apart from these forces we have described, there are also other forces contributing to the de-mythification of the white man in Africa. The presence of independent sovereign African states has had an important role to play in this whole process. There was a time when it looked as though the natural ruler of Africa was not the African, but the white man. History, however, has partly reversed this, and now it looks as though the white man, after all, is not the natural ruler of Africa. The overthrowing of European imperialism in Asia, the United Nations' strong stand against gunpowder diplomacy, the U.S.A. Supreme Court decision to terminate segregation in all public schools, and the powerful voice of India against European imperialism in Africa, have all contributed to this de-mythification going on everywhere in Africa.

There was a time when the white man used to argue thus: It has taken the white man two thousand years to arrive at his present stage of Western civilization, and the African, who has had no civilization to speak of, has no right to clamour for full admission in this civilization until he also has done his stint, that is two thousand years. The African used to accept this for he had no way of refuting it. But suddenly it dawned on his consciousness that, even if he accepted this mathematical proposition of 2,000 years, when he had finished his term of apprenticeship the white man would still say to the African: 'It took the white man 4,000 years to be where he is.' Thus the thinking African sees in the time factor the white man's persistent refusal to share with him the common things of life.

As one African humorously but pointedly said, 'If 2,000 years is the only requirement, that is easy. It has taken us 2,000 years to be where we are, unless the white man assumes that he was created 2,000 years before we were.'

The time factor, which has been one of the strongest arguments the white man has been using, is also losing its impact on the African. Because it has taken one race five centuries to build up an imposing civilization, it does not follow that the next race must take the same period. Every succeeding generation stands on the shoulders of the preceding one, and hence can see further afield than its predecessors, otherwise there would be no such thing as the evolution of the human race. Modern conditions have rendered the time factor almost meaningless.

There was a time when the African used to accept the time-factor argument against him. The absence of an imposing black man's civilization, his little round pole-and-mud huts in Central Africa, and round grass huts in Natal, the half-nakedness found all over Africa, and the lack of modern conveniences in African villages, were pointed out to him again and again in a most convincing manner, and it was said that in view of these backward conditions it would take hundreds of years before he would measure up to Western standards. What is more important, here, is that the African believed it. But he now sees the arguments of the white man shattered to pieces. The illiterate African mothers have given birth to sons who became men of letters; the mud-and-pole hut-keepers, to modern African housewives; the mother who trembles at and runs away from the sound of a car has a son who drives a taxi; the mother who has never travelled beyond a radius of thirty miles from her village has a son who has been around the world; the mother who speaks only one language, spoken by half a million people, has a son or a daughter who speaks a language spoken by many millions of people, and who speaks at least two languages in addition to her own; and millions of African Christians have non-Christian African mothers. The African is deeply impressed to note that many teachers and politicians were born in mud-and-pole huts; that many African lawyers and doctors were goatherds, and that most African business men once belonged to these humble circumstances.

How does an African reconcile the argument that it takes centuries to civilize him when under his very nose there are Africans who have telescoped three centuries in themselves alone? How shall he believe this argument when a Dr. Kwame Nkrumah, born in a bamboo hut, son of a polygynous father, scales the Ghana political peak? More than ever before the African begins to believe that it is not the race, or nation, or tribe, or even a family that matters. In the final analysis it is the individual, black or white, that matters.

For the first time since the occupation of Africa by European powers, the African is beginning to grasp that central fact of life that a man's family, his environment, and his background may help him here and there as he seeks to achieve success, but the real thing that counts is inside the individual himself. It is an unknown factor, indefinable and inaccessible to both the white critic and the African possessor himself. It is this unknown factor that seems to transcend space and time and culture and civilization and thrusts persons of insignificant social stature into the arena of human affairs of great consequence. It is this unknown factor which makes a man raised in a bamboo hut stand his ground in the presence of an opponent raised in a palace.

CHAPTER THIRTEEN

Africa's Challenge

We may be excused if we quote at great length, but we feel compelled to do so so that we may show what happens when a legitimate challenge is not met honestly by powers-that-be. Jomo Kenyatta, the so-called leader of the Mau Mau revolt of 1952-5, described relations between the Kikuyu and the Europeans in Kenya as follows:

'An elephant made friendship with a man. Driven by a heavy thunderstorm, the elephant sought shelter in the man's hut that was on the edge of the forest. The elephant was allowed partial admission, but eventually he evicted the man from his hut and took full possession of the hut, saying: "My dear good friend, your skin is harder than mine, and there is not enough room for both of us, you can afford to remain in the rain while I am protecting my delicate skin from the hailstorm."

'A dispute between the elephant and the man ensued. This attracted the notice of the King of the Jungle. In the interest of peace and good order the Lion assured the grumbling man that he would appoint a Commission of Inquiry: "You have done well by establishing friendship with my people, especially with the elephant who is one of my honourable ministers of state. Do not grumble any more, your hut is not lost to you. Wait until the sitting of my Imperial Commission, and there you will be given plenty of opportunity to state your case. I am sure you will be pleased with the findings of the commission."

'The Commission was duly appointed. It comprised (1) Mr. Rhinoceros; (2) Mr. Buffalo; (3) Mr. Alligator; (4) The Rt. Hon. Mr. Fox to act as chairman; and (5) Mr. Leopard to act as Secretary to the Commission. The man asked that one of his kind be included on the Commission, but he was assured that none of his kind was educated enough to understand the intricacy of jungle law, and that the members of the Commission were God-chosen and would execute their business with justice.

'The elephant gave his evidence: "Gentlemen of the Jungle, there is no need for me to waste your valuable time in relating a story which I am sure you all know. I have always regarded it as my duty to protect the interests of my friends, and this appears to have caused the misunderstanding between myself and my friend here. He invited me to save his hut from being blown away by a hurricane. As the hurricane had gained access owing to the unoccupied space in the hut, I considered it necessary, in my friend's own interests, to turn the undeveloped space to a more economic use by sitting in it myself; a duty which any of you would undoubtedly have performed with equal readiness in similar circumstances."

'Next the man gave interrupted evidence and the Commission delivered its verdict as follows: "In our opinion this dispute has arisen through a regrettable misunderstanding due to the backwardness of your ideas. We consider that Mr. Elephant has fulfilled his sacred duty of protecting your interests. As it is clearly for your good that the space should be put to its economic use, and as you yourself have not yet reached the stage of expansion which would enable you to fill it, we consider it necessary to arrange a compromise to suit both parties. Mr. Elephant shall continue his occupation of your hut, but we give you permission to look for a site where you can build another hut more suited to your needs, and we shall see that you are well protected."

'The man, fearing exposure to the teeth and claws of the members of the Commission, had no alternative. He built another hut. Mr. Rhinoceros came and occupied it. Another Commission of Inquiry was set up. The man was advised to look for a new site. This went on until all the members of the Commission had been properly housed at the expense of the man. Then the desperate man said to himself, "*Ng' enda thi ndeagaga motegi*" (There is nothing that treads on the earth that cannot be trapped, i.e. You can fool people for a time, but not for ever).

'So the man built a big hut, and soon the lords of the jungle came and occupied the big hut. The man shut them in and set the hut on fire and all perished. The man returned home saying: "Peace is costly, but it's worth the expense." [1]

It is interesting to note that the above account was first published in 1938, that is, fourteen years before the Mau Mau Revolt of 1952-5. And in 1952, the Mau Mau did set Kenya on fire in sheer desperation after many British commissions of inquiry had failed to satisfy the Kikuyu. It is also interesting to note that Jomo Kenyatta's *Facing Mount Kenya* is dedicated to:

'Moigoi and Wamboi and all the dispossessed youth of Africa: for perpetuation of communion with ancestral spirits through the fight for African Freedom, and in the firm faith that the dead, the living, and the unborn will unite to rebuild the destroyed shrines.'

Whatever the verdict of history may be for or against Jomo Kenyatta, the truth remains that he embodied the spirit of freedom and independence found all over Africa today. He tried to fight for the Kikuyu to be treated like human beings in the land of their birth. Everything else had failed and a revolution was the only course open to the Kikuyu. The Mau Mau Revolt was the only course open to them.

What we are trying to say here is that if the doors of democracy are deliberately shut against the Africans, some other hideous alternatives will present themselves to them.

I remember a Briton hotly arguing with an African politician. 'You Africans surprise us. Before the white man came to Africa, you never clamoured for these things. You did nothing except sleep.'

'And while we slept we enjoyed our sleep', replied the African.

'I suggest very strongly that you resume your sleep, and stop all this nonsense about African independence.'

'You can't have it both ways', said the African. 'You must accept the consequences of your own actions. Africa is astir and it's impossible to resume our sleep.'

One African thinker put it this way, 'It's no good expecting an awake African to behave as though he was still asleep'.

[1] Jomo Kenyatta: *Facing Mount Kenya* (Secker and Warburg), pp. 47-52.

The sleeping millions of Africa have suddenly found them-selves on the march. Nothing will stop them as long as they themselves are determined to go forward.

I remember talking with my friend Leopold Takawira, now an executive officer of the Capricorn Africa Society which, since it is multiracial in its outlook, is one of the few beacons of hope in multiracial Africa. Takawira was shocked when he found that he was being accused by some of his white friends of ingratitude. This accusation had been made after he had championed strongly the cause of African freedom and independence. 'We invite him to our house', ran the charge, 'and drink tea with him. Then he turns round and talks of African independence. Ungrateful wretch!'

This European attitude is altogether common. How many times has the writer heard missionaries complain, 'We taught him how to read and write, and now he writes us letters complaining', as if to say anyone taught by them should never complain! How often have I heard Europeans complain, 'Before we came here, these natives were naked and half-naked savages. Now they say they want their freedom. Ungrateful brutes!' as if clothing was the purchase price of a people's freedom. Apparently this attitude does not help solve the many problems confronting Africa. Those who serve Africa to secure the submission of the African people are not helping the marching millions of Africa who want to be themselves, and who demand their freedom and independence. Service with imperialistic designs is not the correct answer to Africa's multiracial affairs.

1. AFRICA IS A CHALLENGE TO WESTERN DEMOCRACY. If Africa is denied Western democracy, then it is only natural and right for Africa to forge on the anvil of necessity other political ideo-logies accessible to her. Westerners do not like Africa to go communist, and yet at the same time they do not want Africa to go democratic, since the latter process would liquidate white supremacy. Western democracy in Africa carries in her womb, not democracy, but dictatorship. It is futile, unstatesmanlike, and ridiculous to expect a people who are denied democracy to fight for Western democracy in the event of a crisis. People defend

that which they enjoy, not that which oppresses them. If the African is compelled to live all his life under a European dictatorial system, then when stronger dictators come on the scene he is likely to throw in his lot with whatever dictator promises to carry the day, and this in turn greatly weakens Western democracy. In the event of a new dictator, the African has nothing to lose or to gain. He is only too happy to see his old dictator suffer defeat at the hands of the new one. But let the African have his freedom and independence, and he will fight with his very life against the new dictator because he has something at stake. Why must the African be expected to be loyal to Western democracy if he does not enjoy the democracy he enjoyed before the coming of the white people to Africa? Why must he die so that Western Europe and the U.S.A. may preserve their democracy which he himself does not enjoy? The marching millions of Africa are saying, 'Give us the democracy we know, and the democracy you yourselves know, and you will have real support in us. Don't give us sham democracy.'

The argument that the Africans cannot rule themselves is quite unacceptable. The Africans can rule themselves like any other people in the world. They are not perfect human beings. They have their failings like all other nations. The Western countries often say, 'Unless they [Africans] can assure us that they can rule themselves well, it is extremely dangerous to give them full independence', forgetting that there is not a single Western nation that has a clean record. Under the leadership of the West, the world saw two devastating European wars whose total human destruction stood at 42,000,000. It is only European administration that caused the destruction of human life on a global scale. It is therefore no good excuse to deny the African the right to rule himself on the ground that he cannot rule well, because even Westerners cannot rule themselves well. It is the Western powers and Russia that threaten the human race with extinction. It is a pity that Western democracy does in Africa what Russian communism does in Eastern Europe—that is, rule the people against their will.

I remember the argument between Mr. Thomas Ngara and

a British settler. 'If your people, Mr. Ngara, can prove to us that they can rule themselves well, we will give them their independence', assured the Briton.

Mr. Ngara, becoming intensely heated, replied, 'Why must my people necessarily prove to you that they can rule themselves well? Who are you to whom we must have to prove that we can rule ourselves? Who has given you that right so that 200 million people must prove to you that they can rule themselves well? We don't have to prove that. That is none of your business.'

The problem of democracy in Africa is to spread itself more quickly or else something else will take its place. Africa is asking the Western democratic countries to extend democracy to Africa, but Western democracies are refusing to do so. African nationalism is merely a specific expression of the human spirit seeking freedom and independence, and it is a pity that Western democracies do not quicken African freedom and independence. The challenge Africa issues to the West is: Give us our independence. Help us in our struggle for independence. Our independence is your independence. We are fighting for human freedom. We want to be free people. You do not want Russia to shackle you, but you want to shackle us. You can't have it both ways. Our independence will guarantee that of the rest of mankind. Western democracies, by refusing us democracy, are not playing true.

2. AFRICA IS A CHALLENGE TO THE WHOLE CHRISTIAN CHURCH IN THE WORLD. In the past the Church has played an important part in the opening up and development of Africa. But the Church should not become satisfied with her glorious record of the past and forget about the many needs of today. The Shona proverb is worth remembering, *Mandakadya kare haanyaradze mwana* (That which was eaten long ago cannot quiet the child, i.e. You cannot quiet a child who is crying for candy today by telling him that he had candy a month ago). The Church cannot solve the many problems of today by appealing to her past record. Her past record represents that which was eaten long ago, to use the Shona proverb, and this cannot satisfy the many hungers of the African people who are reaching out for some-

thing that would anchor their lives in the fast-changing conditions of the twentieth century. A sustained effort is absolutely necessary.

(*a*) The Church can meet this challenge in the field of faith. Faith is part and parcel of human life on all levels. The interpretation of the nature and destiny of man depends upon the kind of faith. Hence a Godless faith tends to devalue man, and man is finally held accountable to earthly powers-that-be. The rise of the industrial system, and all that goes with it, has destroyed many religious conceptions which gave content to African life, and has thereby created a religious vacuum among many African communities. A religious vacuum means a state of godlessness, and this in turn threatens African life with hollowness, emptiness and meaninglessness, for indeed, man shall not live by bread alone but by every word which comes from the mouth of God. This was said twenty centuries ago, and it is still true today. There is that hunger for God—for things more abiding.

The question of faith is of vital importance for the emerging Africans. A Hindu intellectual, an Islamic lawyer, a Buddhist scholar, a Jewish business man, and a Christian doctor all practise their religions with pride, but the same thing could not be said of advanced Africans. They tend to abandon their own native religions which did not go beyond ancestor or family worship. The advanced African therefore has two alternatives: either he becomes altogether Godless, or he adopts a new highly organized religion—such as Islam, Hinduism, Buddhism or Christianity—as his own. His own ancestor or family religion, while it served a good purpose in the past, does not seem able to serve his needs today. He needs a religion that is loaded with universalism rather than particularism. In the past he lived in close touch with his ancestors, and hence the highly exclusive ancestor worship served him well. But today he lives in close touch with the world at large, and hence his ancestor worship is no longer satisfying, and hence the crying need for a more satisfying religion. Western industry has uprooted him from his ancestral religion.

(*b*) The Church can meet this challenge in the field of human relations. In the past the Church has helped in breaking down the prejudice of secular powers against appointing deserving

Africans to key positions. It can do still more in this direction in its own right as a Church. By living out the actual principles of the Christian faith, by standing for that which is truly Christian and just, the Church can serve as a lighthouse in Africa's multi-racial ocean of life so that those caught in the raging storms may see the right direction in which to steer the ship *Multiracial* safe into harbour. A guiding star that radiates through and through with the universal brotherhood of man is the crying need in the human relations of Africa. A new way of looking at life, that transcends nationality and race, that only looks at man as man, is an urgent need in multiracial Africa. The Church could be that guiding star, and could provide that new angle of vision which is above race and nationality, if it actually practises, in its own sphere as a Church, the principles of the Gospel as laid down by Christ himself. It is not altogether true to say the unrest in Africa is caused by political, economic, and social tension. Deep down below all this, there is the spiritual ill-health. When one man refuses another political equality, economic equality, and equal human consideration, that could not be rightly said to be a political or economic problem. That is a spiritual problem which needs urgent attention. Our human relations are essentially spiritual. When the human spirit is not favourably disposed towards other human beings, good political, economic, and social relations are almost impossible. Multiracial Africa therefore stands in great need of such institutions as will transform the spirit of man, for man's own good. Multiracial Africa is inflicted with deep wounds of racialism, and it needs the healing hands of the Church.

(c) The Church can meet this challenge in the field of educa-tion. The African child and the African adult are reaching out for thoughts and ideas that may help them as they seek to find their place in the world. There are many ideas and thoughts—worthy and ignoble—beckoning to them with an irresistible persistence. It has been said that thoughts rule the world. We may add that the type of thought the African, the white man and the Asian in multiracial Africa have will determine the future of race and therefore human relations. In the absence of a sound Christian education—that is, that type of education that stresses the sanctity and personality of each individual—a destructive type of education may be resorted to. At least, it is to be recognized that the African is hungry for learning, and he will learn whatever presents itself to him until the right thing comes his way. Neither an anti-white system of education nor a 'keep-down-the-African' type of education is good for multiracial Africa. Here, then, the Church has a wonderful opportunity of disseminating Christian literature and fostering Christian education that is intended for the fullest development, not the suppression, of man. In this era of the emergence of African nationalism and the resurgence of world religions, it is simply imperative that educationally, intellectually, and ideologically the Church should rise to the great occasion, or else it misses the opportunity, and other institutions and forces take care of the situation. In the field of mass literacy, medicine, agriculture, and a chain of other fields, the Church has an untold opportunity of serving the marching millions of Africa, and of sowing effectively the seeds of peace, love, and universal brotherhood of man under the universal Fatherhood of God. That is the challenge today. The Church in Africa and elsewhere has to answer the challenge Africa presents. Give Africa worthy thoughts and ideas, and the marching millions will be a blessing to the rest of mankind. Deprive her of these, and Africa goes down with the rest of mankind. When Germany sank during World War II as a result of wrong thoughts and ideas, the rest of the world sank with her. We can neglect what goes on in one part of the world only at our own risk.

Trade unions, factories, and schools have demonstrated that people of all colours can live and work together. The Church can help tremendously in its own right as a Church to demonstrate practically the deeper spiritual realities that bind all mankind in a bond of common fellowship. If the Church fails to do this, something else will try to do the job. The need of multiracial Africa, as of the rest of the world, is that all peoples of different colours and climes and nationalities shall realize and accept that:

All people of the earth
Share but one common birth,
    One destiny;
One sun shines o'er us all,
Alike we rise and fall,
One night will spread its pall
    Eternally.

so that together they may sincerely pray:

Great God of all the earth,
Lead us to know the worth
    Of sympathy;
May fellowship increase,
May all contention cease,
O may we dwell in peace
    And unity.[1]

[1] Leonard B. McWhood.